Teach Yourself Origami

Teach Yourself Origami

John Montroll

Dover Publications, Inc.
New York

To Søren, Pauline, Sine, Elizabeth, and Natasha

Published in Canada by General Publishing Company, Ltd., 30
Lesmill Road, Don Mills, Toronto, Ontario.
Published in the United Kingdom by Constable and Company,
Ltd., 3 The Lanchesters, 162–164 Fulham Palace Road, London
W6 9ER.

Bibliographical Note

This work is first published in 1998 in separate editions by Antroll
Publishing Company, Maryland, and Dover Publications, Inc.,
New York.

Library of Congress Cataloging-in-Publication Data

Montroll, John.
   Teach yourself origami / by John Montroll.
      p.   cm.
   ISBN 0-486-40141-3 (pbk.)
   1. Origami. I. Title.
TT870.M574   1998
736'.982—dc21
                                           98-2563
                                          CIP

Manufactured in the United States of America
Dover Publications, Inc., 31 East 2nd Street, Mineola, N.Y. 11501

Introduction

*W*elcome to the wonderful and magic world of origami. This collection teaches the new folder how to get started in origami and to systematically aquire more skills. The first part of the book introduces techniques and maneuvers, and builds upon them using simple models as examples. Intermediate and advanced models are gradually added, and students quickly find themselves origami masters.

This book can also be used as a text or lesson plan for individuals, schools or origami courses. Start from the beginning of the book, and fold through it, one model at a time. Diagram symbols, techniques, and terminology are introduced progressively, and each model builds upon the skills aquired in completing prior ones.

Every model has been tested by novices. Nothing included here is impossible, but some areas require practice to perfect. If you find a new technique especially difficult to acquire, persevere. Start again from the beginning, or put the model aside and try again later.

There are many styles of origami, and many approaches. In this book I have included only models which can be folded from one uncut square. Some of the origami in the first chapter is traditional, and two pieces in the advanced chapter were created by Fred Rohm, an American origami pioneer. Any models without credit are my designs.

As in all my books, the illustrations conform to the internationally accepted Randlett-Yoshizawa conventions. These symbols are used in most recently published diagrams, so learning them will open the pages of other origami books, too.

The colored side of origami paper is represented by the shadings in the diagrams. Origami paper can be found in many hobby shops or purchased by mail from OrigamiUSA, 15 West 77th Street, New York, NY 10024-5192 or from Dover Publications, Inc., 31 East 2nd Street, Mineola, NY 11501. Large sheets are easier to use than small ones.

Many people helped make this book possible. I wish to thank Beth Maccallum for introducing Fred Rohm's models to me, and Krista Willett for introducing them to Beth. Special thanks to Bea Rohm for her permission to use Fred's models. I would also like to thank Jan Polish for her work as editor. Of course I also thank the many folders who proof-read the diagrams.

John Montroll

Contents

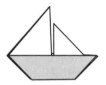

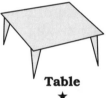

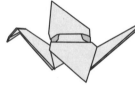

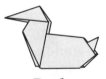

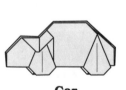
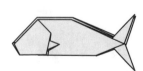

Swan
★★
page 54

Toucan
★★
page 57

Anhinga
★★
page 60

Lily
★★
page 63

Crane
★★
page 66

Canary
★★
page 69

Dragon
★★
page 72

Pig
★★
page 75

Cat
★★
page 78

Boar
★★
page 81

Lion
★★
page 85

Camel
★★
page 89

Chapter 3: Advanced

**Fred Rohm's
Impossible Vase**
★★★
page 96

**Fred Rohm's
Water Wheel**
★★★
page 100

Deer
★★★
page 105

Elephant
★★★
page 109

Bee
★★★
page 116

Symbols

Lines

— — — — — — — Valley fold, fold in front.

—·—··—·—··—··— Mountain fold, fold behind.

———————— Crease line.

··· X-ray or guide line.

Arrows

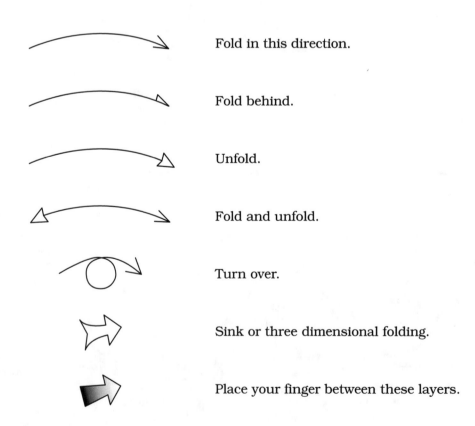

Fold in this direction.

Fold behind.

Unfold.

Fold and unfold.

Turn over.

Sink or three dimensional folding.

Place your finger between these layers.

Chapter 1—Beginner

Getting Started

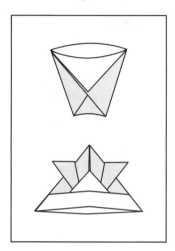

Pull Out

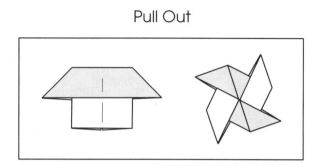

Squash Fold

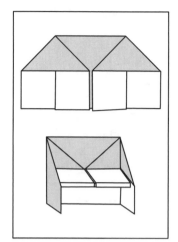

Someone who has not folded can learn the basics from this chapter. New techniques are shown one at a time, along with several traditional Japanese models. There are even a few practice models.

When you fold something for the first time it could seem difficult. If you do have trouble, fold very slowly and carefully and do not give up. Once you have managed something new, fold it again to see how much easier it becomes.

Preliminary Fold

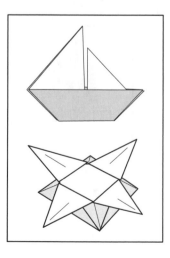

Waterbomb Base

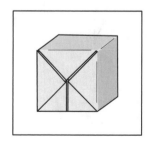

Blintz Fold

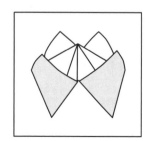

Petal Fold

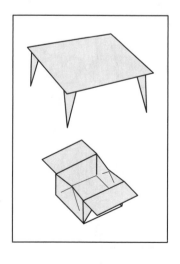

Bird Base

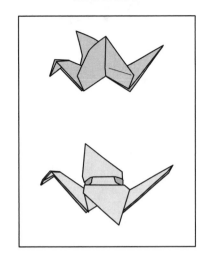

Frog Base

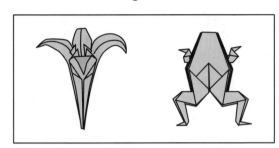

Reverse Fold

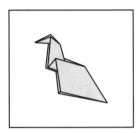

The models shown are meant to teach a new maneuver one at a time. It would be better not to skip any of the models. After the completion of the chapter you will have folded the waterbomb (balloon), famous crane, frog, and many other traditional favorites along with a few of my own.

Outside Reverse Fold

Rabbit Ear

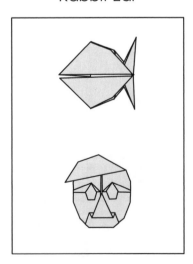

Sink

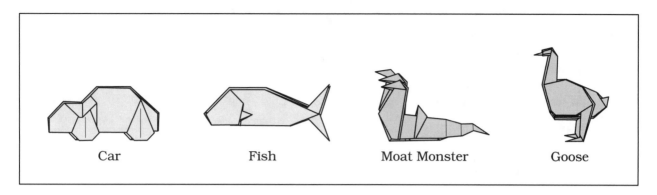

Car   Fish   Moat Monster   Goose

Following the diagrams:

1. Origami paper is colored on one side, white on the other. The shading in the diagrams represents the colored side. In the first step of each model, check which side begins face up.

2. In each step, check for the kind of folds being done, along with possible landmarks.

3. Make sure you look at the next step to see what the folds will become.

4. Hold your paper exactly as shown in the diagram, note any instructions to turn over or rotate the model.

5. Be sure not to skip steps. It is perhaps the most common mistake.

Structures and Bases

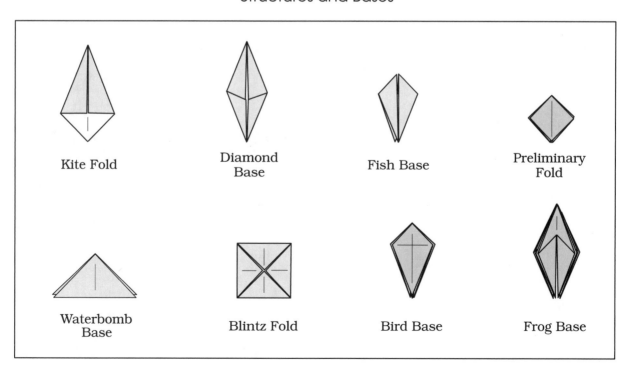

Kite Fold   Diamond Base   Fish Base   Preliminary Fold

Waterbomb Base   Blintz Fold   Bird Base   Frog Base

Getting Started

New Symbols:

Valley fold line (dash dash dash...),
fold in front along the line.

– – – – – – – – – – – –

Fold in the direction of the arrow.

Mountain fold line (dash dot dot dash...),
fold behind along the line.

– · · – · · – · · – · ·

Fold behind.

Crease line, an existing fold in the paper.

Unfold.

●   Dot, used for landmarks.

Cup Traditional

For the first model, all of the new symbols are
used. Every step uses landmarks so each fold
is given an exact location. It is often fun to
fold a model a few times and memorize it; this
helps the folding to become automatic.

1

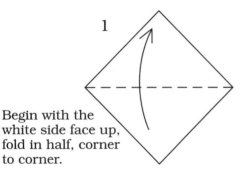

Begin with the
white side face up,
fold in half, corner
to corner.

2

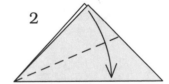

Though the corners at the top
should meet, they are
separated in the diagram for
clarity. Fold one side down.

3

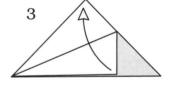

Unfold.

4

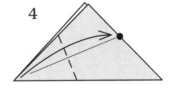

Fold the corner to the dot.

5

Fold the other corner.

6

Fold one layer down.

7

Fold behind along
the mountain fold
line.

8

Place your
finger inside to
open the cup.

9

Cup

Hat Traditional

For this model, a few folds are done without landmarks. This means that you can change the angle or position of these folds so that each hat will be different.

New Symbol:

Turn over.

1

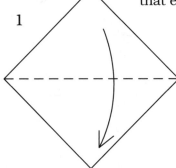

Begin with the white side up. Fold in half.

2

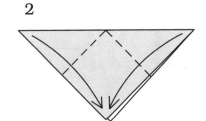

Fold the corners down, one at a time, to meet at the bottom.

3

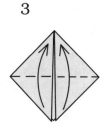

Fold the corners up, one at a time.

4

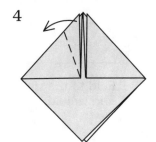

Fold a corner so it sticks out. There is no landmark.

5

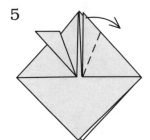

Repeat on the other side.

6

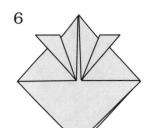

Turn over.

7

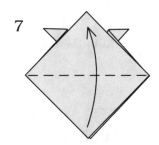

Fold one layer up.

8

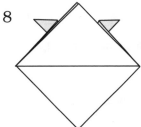

9

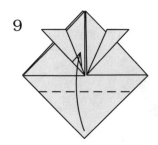

There are no landmarks.

10

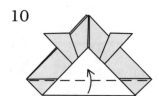

11

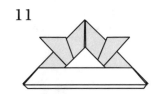

Place your finger inside to open the hat.

12

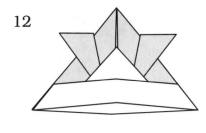

Hat

Pull Out

The concept of pulling out comes in many forms. Sometimes the results can be surprising. Look carefully at the direction of the arrow and at the next step.

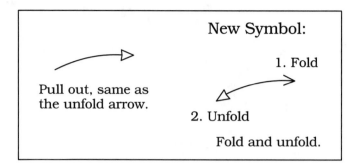

New Symbol:

Pull out, same as the unfold arrow.

1. Fold

2. Unfold

Fold and unfold.

House Traditional

This simple model gives an example of pulling out a corner. It begins with pre-creasing.

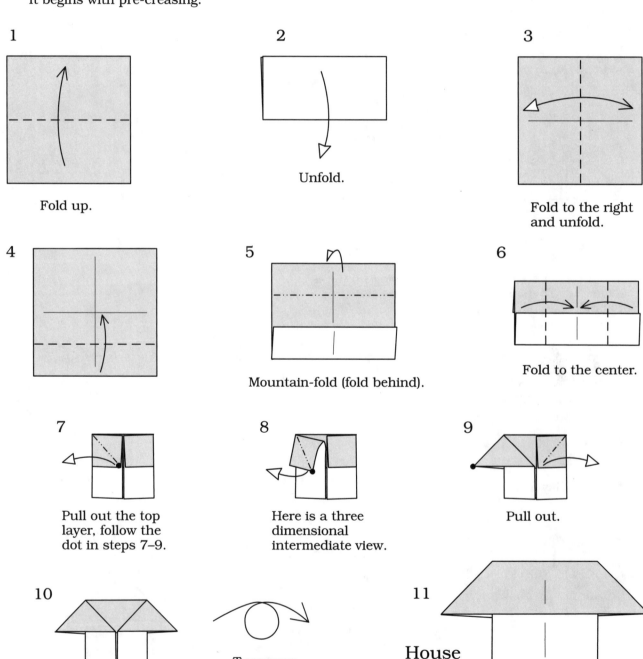

1

Fold up.

2

Unfold.

3

Fold to the right and unfold.

4

5

Mountain-fold (fold behind).

6

Fold to the center.

7

Pull out the top layer, follow the dot in steps 7–9.

8

Here is a three dimensional intermediate view.

9

Pull out.

10

Turn over.

11

House

Pin Wheel Traditional

For this example all four corners will be pulled out. Like the house, it begins with pre-creasing.

1

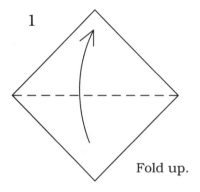

Fold up.

2

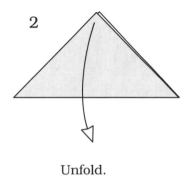

Unfold.

3

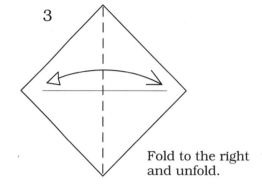

Fold to the right and unfold.

4

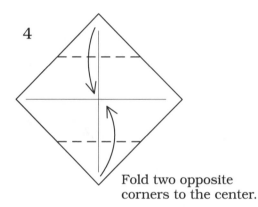

Fold two opposite corners to the center.

5

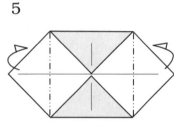

Fold the corners behind.

6

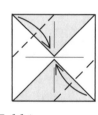

Fold two corners to the center.

7

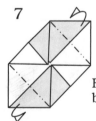

Fold the corners behind.

8

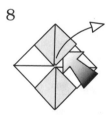

Place your finger inside to pull out the corner.

9

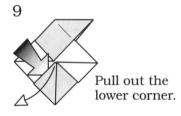

Pull out the lower corner.

10

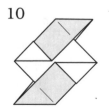

11

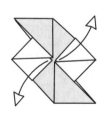 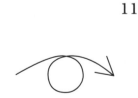

Pull out the white corners.

12

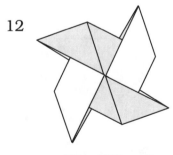

Pin Wheel

Pull Out 15

Squash Fold

In a squash fold, some paper is opened and then made flat. It is usually indicated with a mountain fold line, and often accompanied by the large shaded arrow showing where to place your finger. The text will usually mention the squash fold.

Many Squash Folds Practice Model

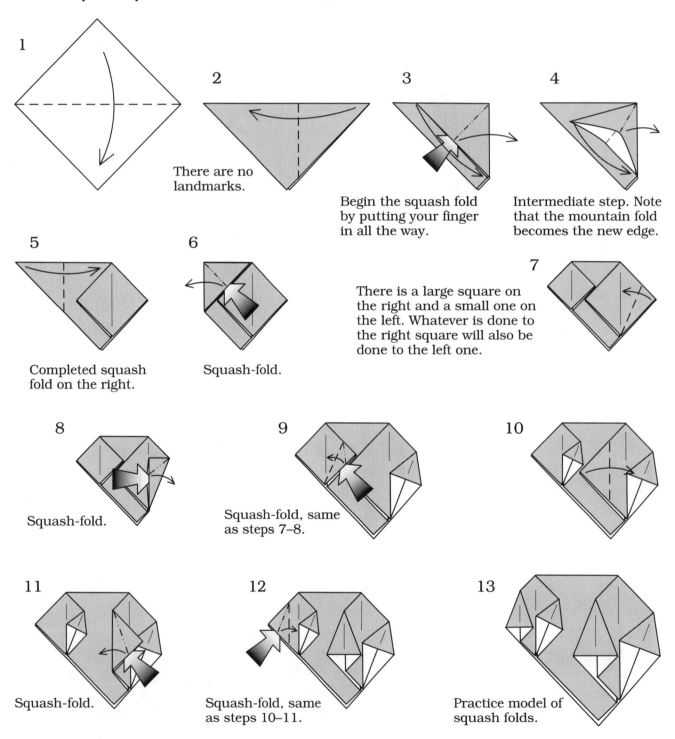

1

2

There are no landmarks.

3

Begin the squash fold by putting your finger in all the way.

4

Intermediate step. Note that the mountain fold becomes the new edge.

5

Completed squash fold on the right.

6

Squash-fold.

7

There is a large square on the right and a small one on the left. Whatever is done to the right square will also be done to the left one.

8

Squash-fold.

9

Squash-fold, same as steps 7–8.

10

11

Squash-fold.

12

Squash-fold, same as steps 10–11.

13

Practice model of squash folds.

House Traditional

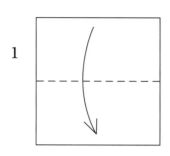

1

Fold in half.

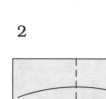

2

Fold in half.

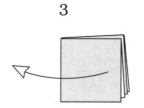

3

Unfold.

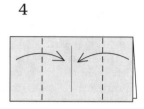

4

Fold to the center.

5

Place your finger
inside for this
squash fold.

6

Continue opening
the model, pushing
down on the top.

7

Squash-fold.

8

House

Piano Traditional

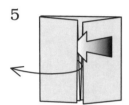

1

Begin with the house.

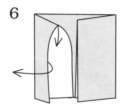

2

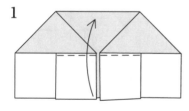

3

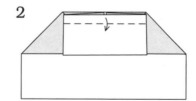

4

Open.

5

Piano

Preliminary Fold

The preliminary fold is the beginning shape of thousands of origami designs. It is named because two bases, the bird base and frog base, are folded from it. Two folding methods are given, though method 2 provides the preliminary fold in a more accurate manner. If you fold the preliminary folds using each method, you will be ready to begin the next two models. Throughout the book, the preliminary fold will be diagrammed as shown to the right.

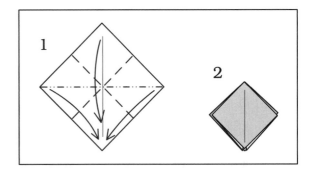

Method 1—Uses squash folds.

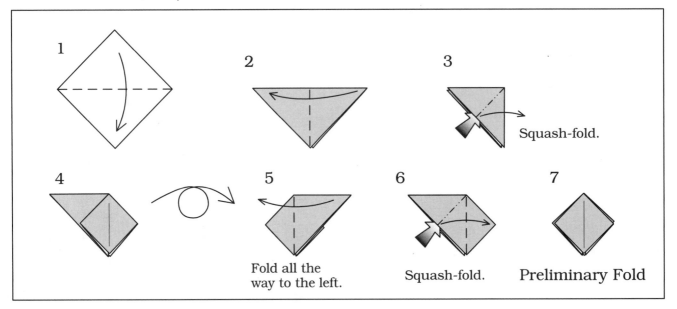

Squash-fold.

Fold all the way to the left.

Squash-fold.

Preliminary Fold

Method 2—Uses fold and unfold.

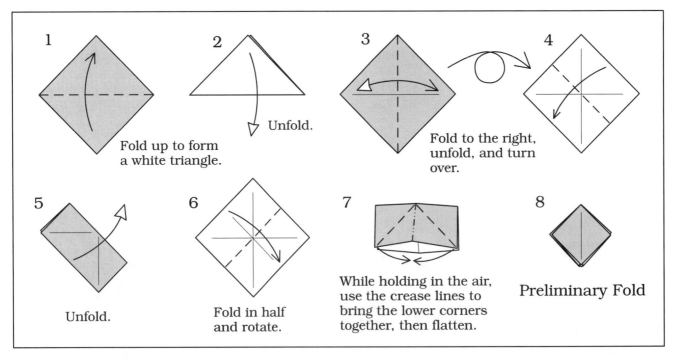

Fold up to form a white triangle.

Unfold.

Fold to the right, unfold, and turn over.

Unfold.

Fold in half and rotate.

While holding in the air, use the crease lines to bring the lower corners together, then flatten.

Preliminary Fold

Sailboat Traditional

This sailboat is the logo for *OrigamiUSA*. Note the jagged arrow in step 7. This indicates the different directions the paper will go.

1

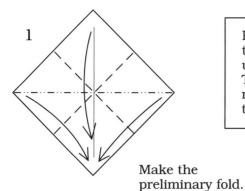

Make the
preliminary fold.

Review of method 2 for making the preliminary fold: Fold and unfold to make white triangles. Turn over, fold and unfold to make colored rectangles. Bring the corners together.

2

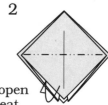

To fold inside, open the model. Repeat behind.

3

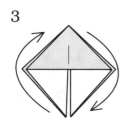

Rotate.

4

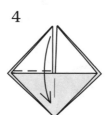

5

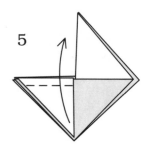

6

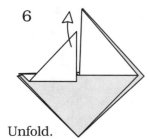

Unfold.

7

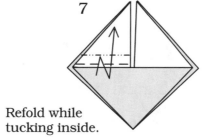

Refold while tucking inside.

8

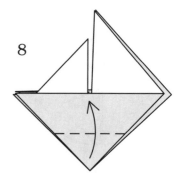

9

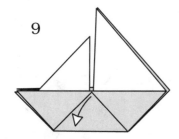

Fold the triangle down a little so the sailboat can stand.

10

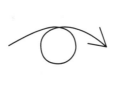

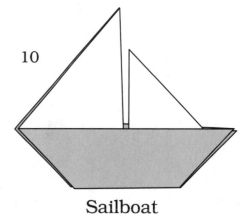

Sailboat

Candy Dish Traditional

This model introduces a maneuver called the minor miracle (step 8). This fold is like turning pages of a book.

1

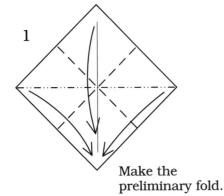

Make the preliminary fold.

2

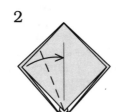

3

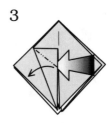

Squash-fold.

4

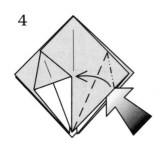

Squash-fold.

5

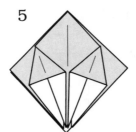

6

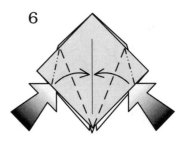

Squash folds.

7

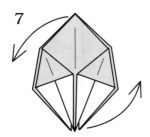

Rotate.

8

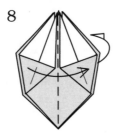

Minor miracle: Fold a layer to the right. Repeat behind. Note that the front and back become hidden while the sides become the front and back in a minor miracle.

9

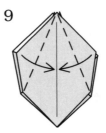

Repeat behind.

10

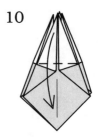

Repeat behind.

11

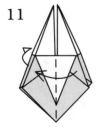

Minor miracle.

12

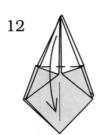

Repeat behind.

13

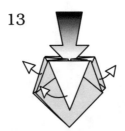

Open and flatten the bottom.

14

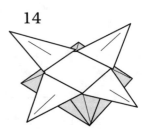

Candy Dish

Waterbomb Base

The waterbomb base is called that because the waterbomb balloon is made from it, along with lots of other models. It is the same as the preliminary fold folded inside-out. To show this, fold a white preliminary fold with the colors on the inside. You can do this by reversing the color instructions while following the directions for the preliminary fold on page 16. Then unfold the preliminary fold, turn it inside-out, and refold it. See if you can make the waterbomb base without making any new folds. Throughout the book the waterbomb base will be diagrammed as shown to the right.

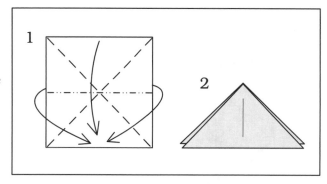

Waterbomb Base

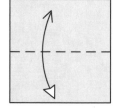

Fold up and unfold.

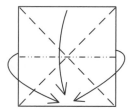

Fold and unfold.

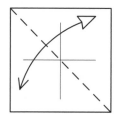

Fold and unfold.

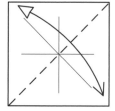

Fold and unfold.

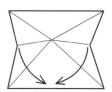

Collapse along the creases.

A three dimensional intermediate step.

Waterbomb Base

Waterbomb Traditional

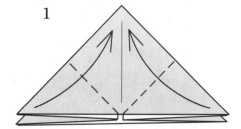

Begin with the waterbomb base. Fold the corners up. Repeat behind.

Fold one layer down and unfold.

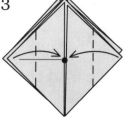

Fold to the center. Repeat behind.

4

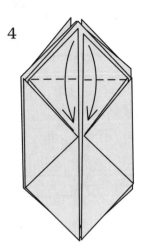

Fold to the center. Repeat behind.

5

Fold along the edge of the existing top layers. Repeat behind.

6

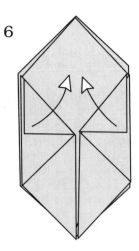

Unfold. Repeat behind.

7

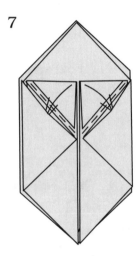

Tuck inside the pockets. Repeat behind.

8

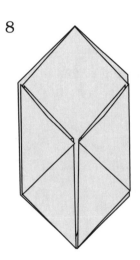

Holding the model like a star, with your fingers between the layers, blow into the bottom.

9

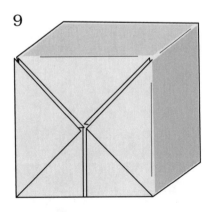

Waterbomb

Blintz Fold

In a blintz fold, the four corners are folded to the center to make a smaller square with more points. Using the additional points, more points are then available to fold. Many things folded from a square can be folded from the blintz fold.

Blintz Fold

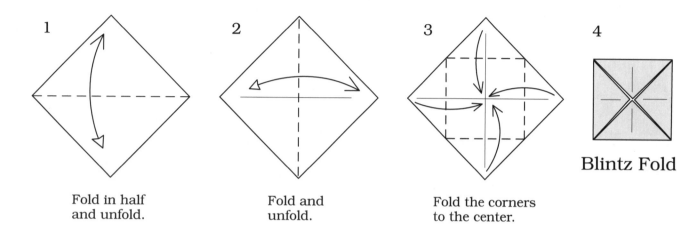

1

Fold in half and unfold.

2

Fold and unfold.

3

Fold the corners to the center.

4

Blintz Fold

Fortune Teller Traditional

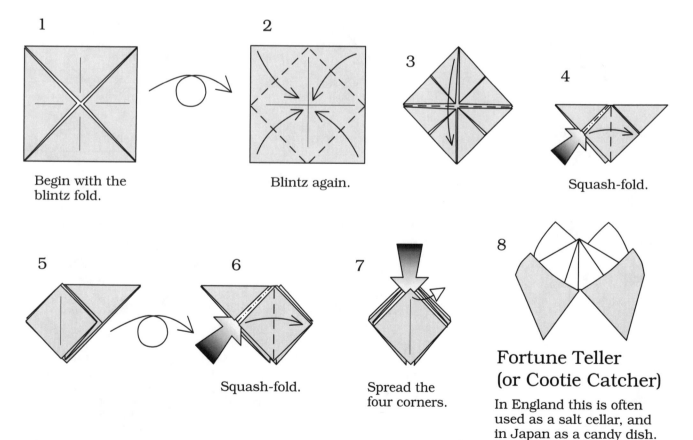

1

Begin with the blintz fold.

2

Blintz again.

3

4

Squash-fold.

5

6

Squash-fold.

7

Spread the four corners.

8

Fortune Teller (or Cootie Catcher)

In England this is often used as a salt cellar, and in Japan as a candy dish.

Petal Fold

In a petal fold, a layer is lifted up, opened, and then flattened. It often follows a squash fold. Generally, there will be two mountain fold lines and one valley fold line.

Two Petal Folds Practice Model

1
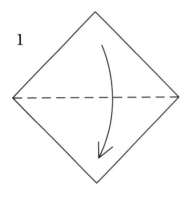

2
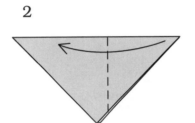

3
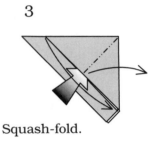

Squash-fold.

4
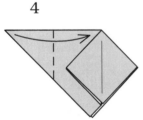

Completed squash fold on the right.

5
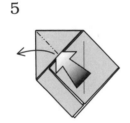

Squash-fold.

6

Squash-fold.

7
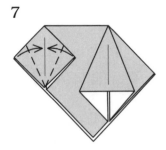

Fold to the center.

8
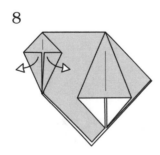

Unfold.

9
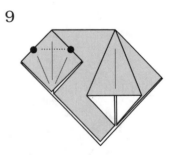

At the moment there is no line between the dots. Imagine that line, shown as a dotted line. That is where you will fold. When you start to fold, concentrate on forming that line, and the rest of the folds will fall into place.

10

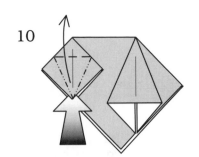

Lift the top layer up, forming a new fold only on that imaginary line, now shown as a valley fold. You will be changing the direction of the two other folds in the top layer, but not forming any folds that are not already in the paper. The completed petal fold is shown in step 13.

11

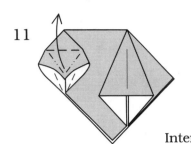

12

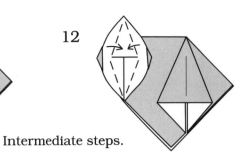

Intermediate steps.

13

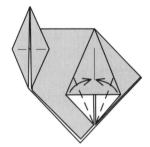

Fold to the center.

14

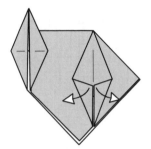

Unfold.

15

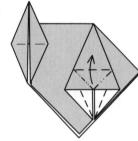

Petal-fold. Begin by folding only on the imaginary line shown as a valley fold line.

16

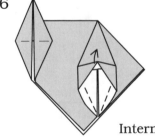

Intermediate step.

17

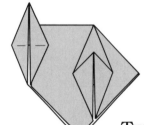

Two petal folds

Table Traditional

1

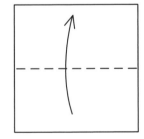

Fold up.

2

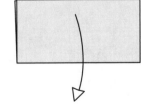

Unfold.

3

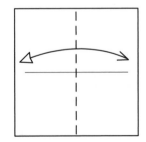

Fold to the right and unfold.

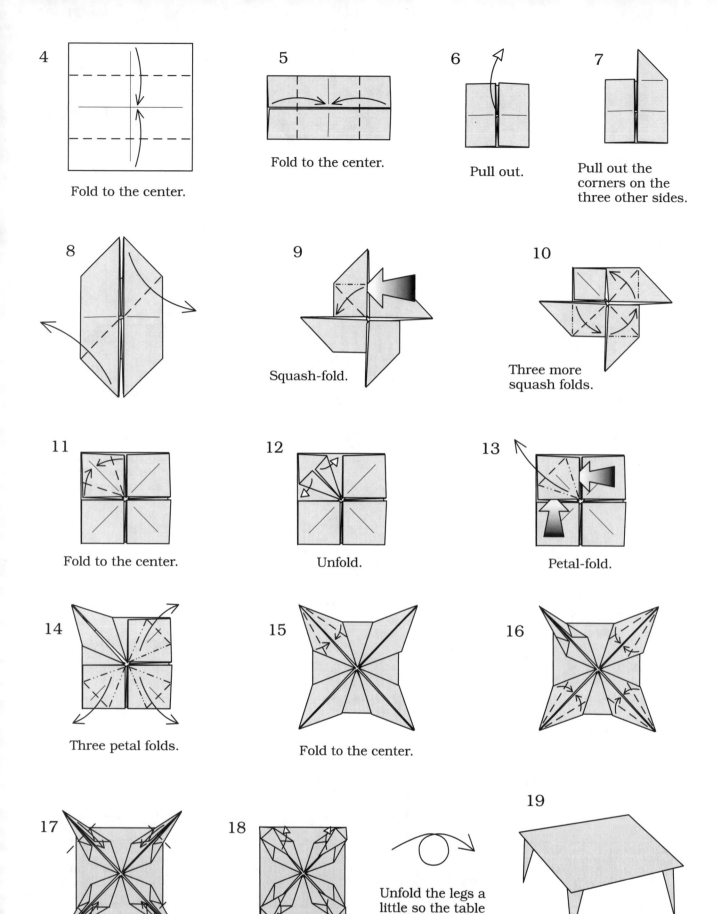

4 Fold to the center.

5 Fold to the center.

6 Pull out.

7 Pull out the corners on the three other sides.

8

9 Squash-fold.

10 Three more squash folds.

11 Fold to the center.

12 Unfold.

13 Petal-fold.

14 Three petal folds.

15 Fold to the center.

16

17

18

Unfold the legs a little so the table can stand.

19 Table

Box Variation of the traditional box

The traditional box is from a rectangle. For this box, a method of dividing into thirds is shown. This gives another example of the petal fold.

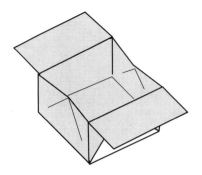

1

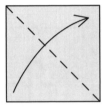

Fold in half.

2

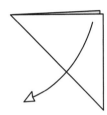

Unfold.

3

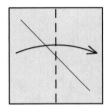

Fold in half.

4

5

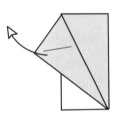

Unfold.

6

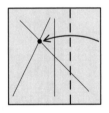

Fold to the dot. This divides the paper into thirds.

7

8

9

10

Mountain-fold (fold behind) in half.

11

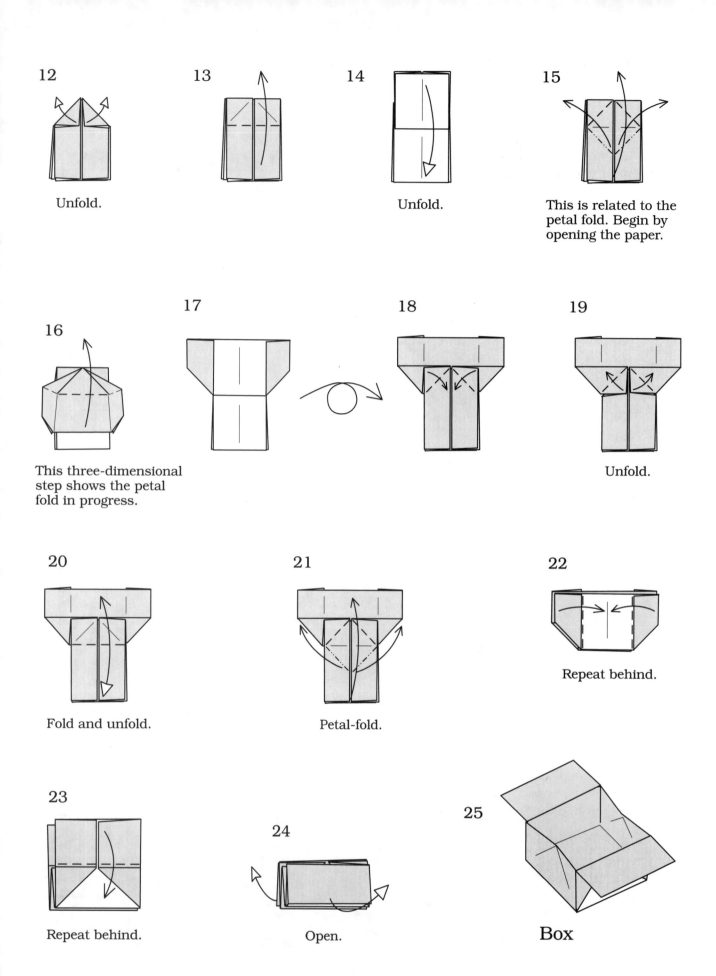

12

Unfold.

13

14

Unfold.

15

This is related to the petal fold. Begin by opening the paper.

16

This three-dimensional step shows the petal fold in progress.

17

18

19

Unfold.

20

Fold and unfold.

21

Petal-fold.

22

Repeat behind.

23

Repeat behind.

24

Open.

25

Box

Inside Reverse Fold

A reverse fold is harder to explain than it is to do. In an inside reverse fold, an end of the paper is folded so that it is between the front and back layers. The model is slightly unfolded for this manuever. There is also an outside reverse fold, to be shown later. The inside reverse fold is much more common, however, and is often called a reverse fold. In addition to the inside reverse fold, the kite fold is introduced.

Two Reverse Folds Practice Model

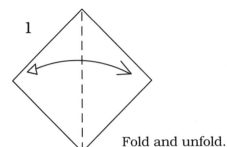

1

Fold and unfold.

2

This is called a kite fold since step 3 looks like a kite.

3

4

Place your finger inside and push the top of the model in the direction of the arrow. The completed fold is shown in step 6.

5

A three dimensional intermediate step.

6

Reverse-fold the bottom inside.

7

Peacock Traditional

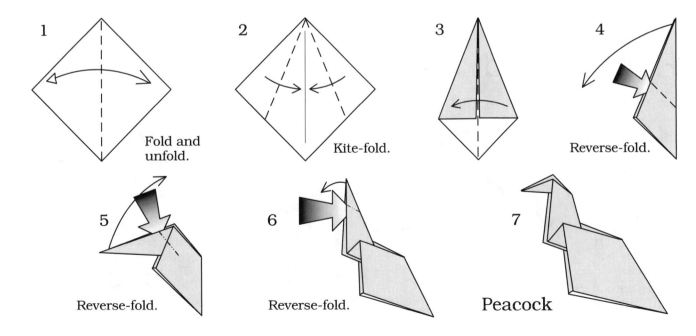

1

Fold and unfold.

2

Kite-fold.

3

4

Reverse-fold.

5

Reverse-fold.

6

Reverse-fold.

7

Peacock

Bird Base

The bird base is possibly the most popular starting point in origami. It is used in thousands of designs. Two of the best known models that begin with the bird base are the flapping bird and crane.

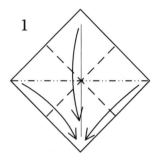

1

Make the preliminary fold.

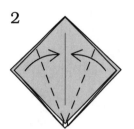

2

Kite-fold. Repeat behind.

3

Fold and unfold.

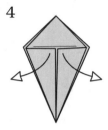

4

Unfold, repeat behind.

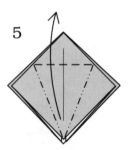

5

Petal-fold.

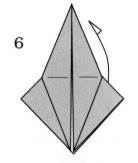

6

Petal-fold behind, i.e. turn over and petal-fold.

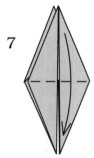

7

Repeat behind.

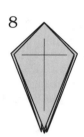

8

Bird Base

Though this is the bird base, models often begin with step 7.

Flapping Bird Traditional

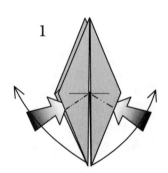

1

Begin with step 7 of the bird base. Reverse folds.

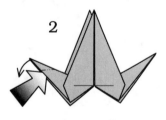

2

Reverse-fold.

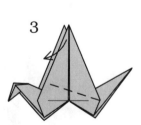

3

Fold the wing out. Repeat behind.

Flapping Bird

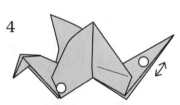

4

Pull the tail back and forth while holding at the bottom of the neck. The wings will flap. The white circles show where to hold.

Crane Traditional

This is perhaps the most famous model in all of origami. The crane symbolizes peace and hope; a thousand cranes, often strung together, are folded for many occasions. Many Japanese children know this model. Being able to fold it is a milestone.

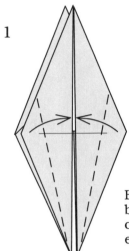

1

Begin with step 7 of the bird base. For this kite fold, fold close to the center line but not exactly on it. Repeat behind.

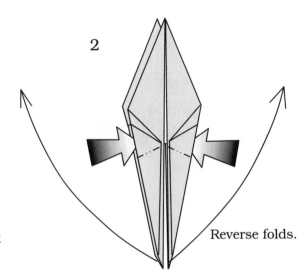

2

Reverse folds.

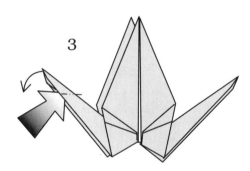

3

Reverse-fold.

4

Pull the wings apart and let the body open.

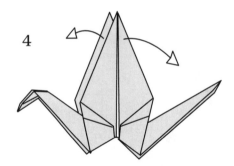

5

Crane

Frog Base

The frog base is named for the jumping frog folded from it. It starts from the preliminary fold.

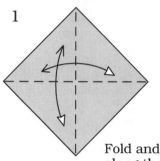

1

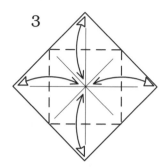

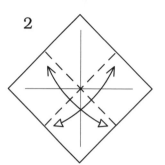

2

3

Fold and unfold along the diagonals.

Fold and unfold.

Blintz fold and unfold.

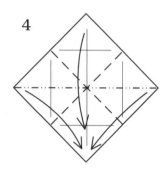

4

5

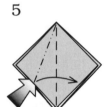

6

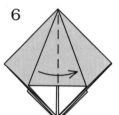

7

Make the preliminary fold.

Squash-fold. Repeat behind.

Repeat behind.

Squash-fold. Repeat behind.

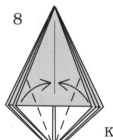

8

9

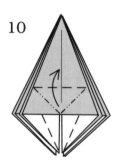

10

Petal-fold. Repeat behind. Recall that to begin the petal fold, you fold along the upper valley fold line.

Kite-fold. Repeat behind.

Unfold. Repeat behind.

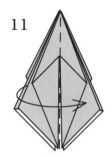

11

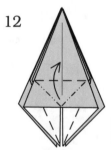

12

13

Repeat behind. This is the minor miracle.

Petal-fold. Repeat behind.

Frog Base

Lily Traditional

This traditional model makes for a beautiful three dimensional flower. Later, a similar lily will be shown with five petals.

1

Begin with the frog base. Fold the loose flap down. Repeat behind.

2
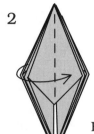
Fold two layers. Repeat behind.

3

Repeat behind.

4

Fold one layer. Repeat behind.

5

Repeat behind.

6
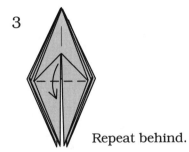
Minor miracle.

7

Repeat behind.

8

Rotate.

9
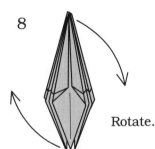
Separate and curl the petals.

10
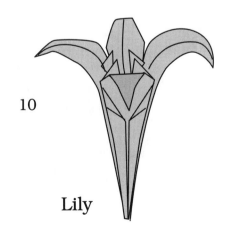
Lily

Frog Traditional

If you push the back of this
traditional jumping frog, it will jump.

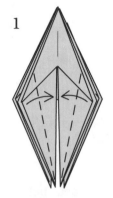

1

Begin with the frog
base. Fold the top
layer. Repeat behind.

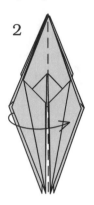

2

Minor miracle.

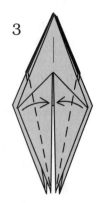

3

Repeat behind.

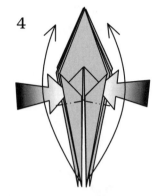

4

There are four points at
the bottom. Reverse fold
the upper two.

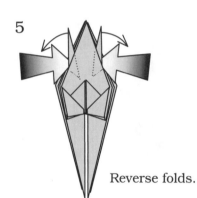

5

Reverse folds.

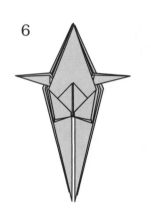

6

7

Reverse folds.

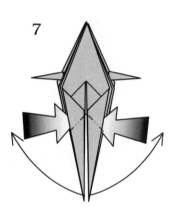

8

Reverse folds.

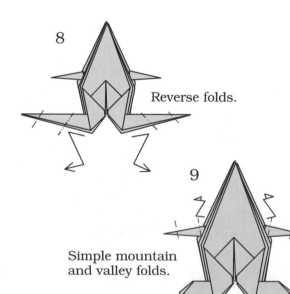

Simple mountain
and valley folds.

9

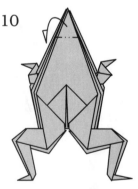

10

Fold behind.

11

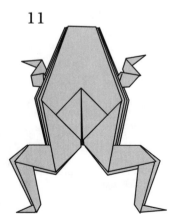

Frog

Outside Reverse Fold

For an outside reverse fold, two layers are folded around themselves. To do so, much of the model is unfolded, and the paper is gently pulled into its new position. You will feel strain in the paper, but it need not rip. Diagrams usually show a valley fold line, and often two arrows indicating that the paper will wrap around itself.

Duck

1

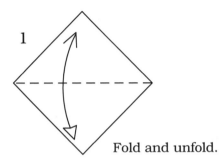

Fold and unfold.

2

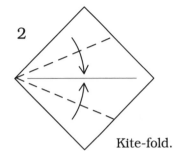

Kite-fold.

3

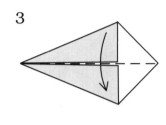

4

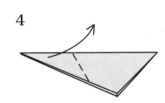

5

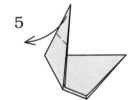

6

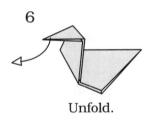

Unfold.

7

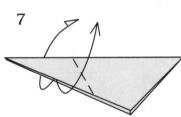

Outside-reverse-fold along the crease. Begin by unfolding and turning the paper around. Step 9 shows the completed fold.

8

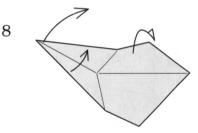

A three dimensional intermediate step.

9

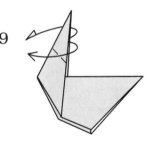

Outside-reverse-fold.

10

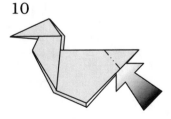

Reverse-fold.

11

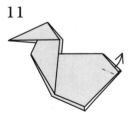

Reverse-fold.

12

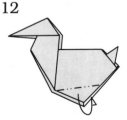

Repeat behind.

13

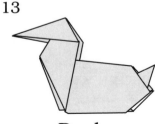

Duck

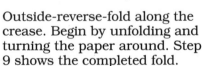

Swan Traditional

1
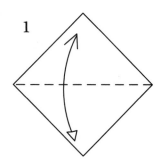

Fold and unfold.

2
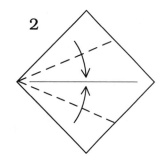

Kite-fold.

3
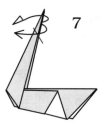

4
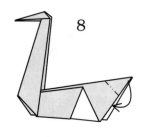

5

Fold in half.

6
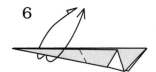

Outside-reverse-fold.

7
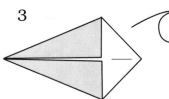

Outside-reverse-fold.

8
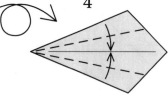

Reverse-fold.

9
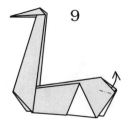

Reverse-fold.

10
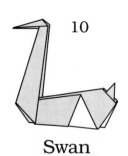

Swan

Penguin

1
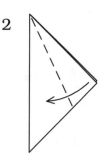

2
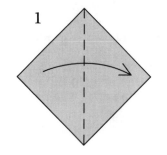

Repeat behind.

3

Reverse-fold.

4

Repeat behind.

5
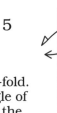

Outside-reverse-fold. See how the angle of the head affects the penguin.

6
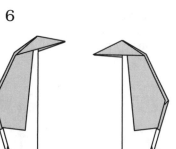

Anxious   Proud   Content

Penguins

Rabbit-Ear

In a rabbit ear fold, a corner of the paper is pinched in half to form a new point which looks somewhat like a rabbit's ear. In the drawings, there are three valley fold lines and one mountain fold line, as in step 6 below. Normally the valley folds are pre-creased, and the mountain fold is made while forming the rabbit ear. A fish base is made from two rabbit ears.

Fish Base

1
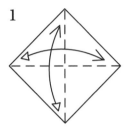
Fold and unfold.

2
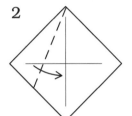
Fold and unfold.

3
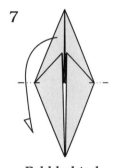
Squash-fold.

4
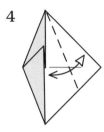
Fold and unfold.

5
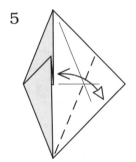
Fold and unfold.

6
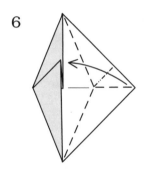
Fold a rabbit ear.
The results are the
same as on the left.

7

Fold behind.

8
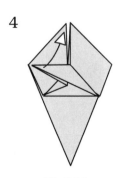
Fish Base

Fish Traditional

1
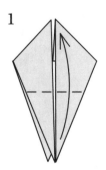
Begin with the
fish base.

2
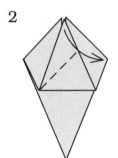

3
Squash-fold.

4
Unfold.

5

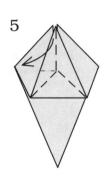

Refold. This is
a rabbit ear.

6

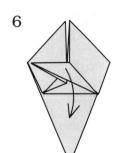

7

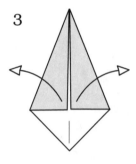

Rabbit-ear behind
and rotate.

8

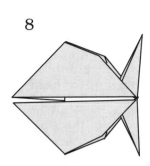

Fish

Face

1

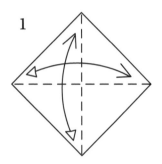

Fold and unfold.

2

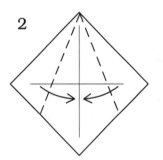

Kite-fold.

3

Unfold.

4

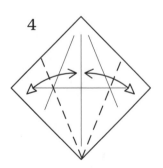

Fold and unfold.

5

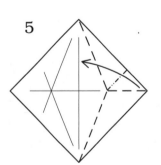

Rabbit-ear.

6

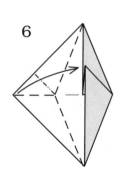

Rabbit-ear.

7

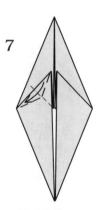

Rabbit-ear.

8

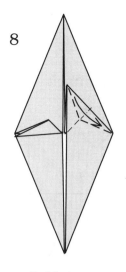

Rabbit-ear.

9

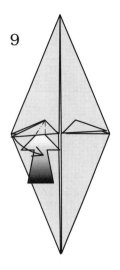

Squash-fold.

10

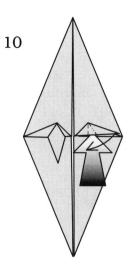

Squash-fold.

11

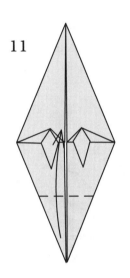

12

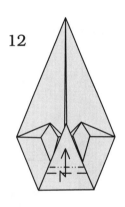

Recall that the jagged arrow shows the directions to fold the paper.

13

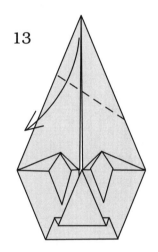

14

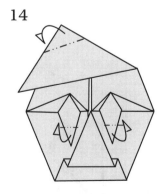

15

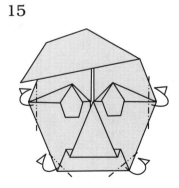

16

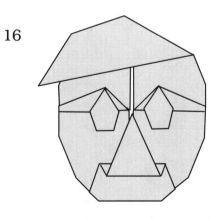

Face

Crimp Fold

A crimp fold is a combination of two reverse folds folded together. They can create a variety of angles and curves; several examples are shown below. Normally you will open the model slightly to form the crimp evenly on each side.

New Symbol:

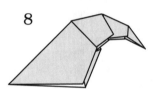

Push in.

Crimp Folds I

1
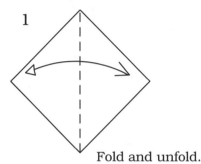
Fold and unfold.

2
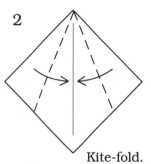
Kite-fold.

3
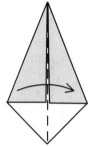

4

Begin a crimp fold.

5
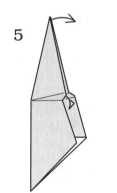
A three-dimensional intermediate step.

6

Crimp-fold.

7

Crimp-fold.

8
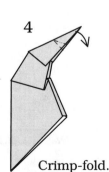

Crimp Folds II

1
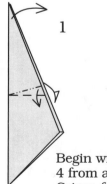
Begin with step 4 from above. Crimp-fold.

2

A three-dimensional intermediate step.

3
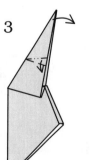
Crimp-fold.

4
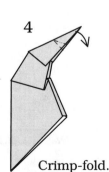
Crimp-fold.

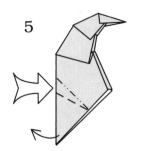

5

Crimp-fold. This is similar to the reverse folds in the duck's tail.

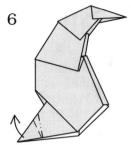

6

Crimp-fold.

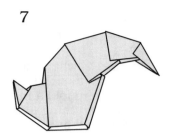

7

Crimp Folds III

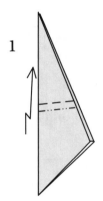

1

Begin with step 4 from above. Crimp-fold.

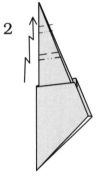

2

More crimp folds, then rotate.

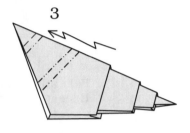

3

More crimp folds.

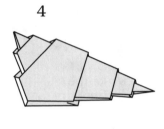

4

Duck and Swan   continued from pages 35 and 36—to add finishing touches

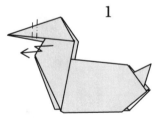

1

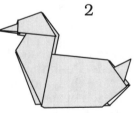

2

Form the beaks with crimp folds.

1

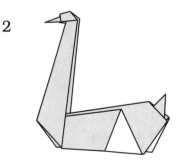

2

Sink

A sink fold is when the center of the paper is folded inside.
Much of the model is unfolded to accomplish the sink. Do not
be afraid to unfold a model. With all the creases it is very easy
to refold everything quickly. In the diagrams there will be a
mountain fold line along with a push in arrow.

Sink Practice Model

1

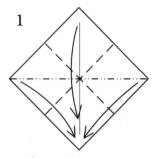

Make the
preliminary fold.

2

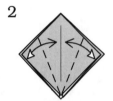

Fold and unfold.
Repeat behind.

3

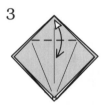

Fold and unfold.

4

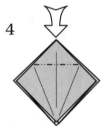

Open the
model to sink.

5

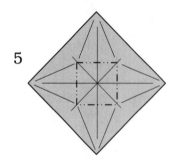

The lines in the center square are valley
and mountain folds. Make them all become
mountain folds. Push the center down into
the model. Note that you are changing the
direction of each of the folds in the center
section so that they can fit inside.

6

Star

1

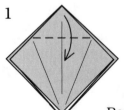

Begin with step 3
from above.

2

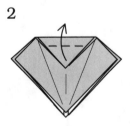

3

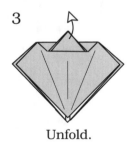

Unfold.

4

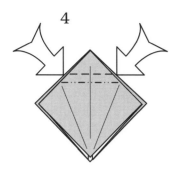

Open the model to
sink down and up.

5

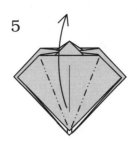

Petal-fold.
Repeat behind.

6

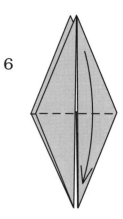

Repeat behind.

7

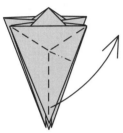

Rabbit-ear.
Repeat behind.

8

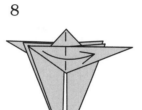

Minor miracle.

9

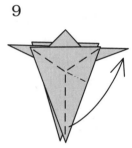

Rabbit-ear.
Repeat behind.

10

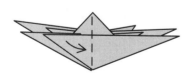

Separate the sides.

11

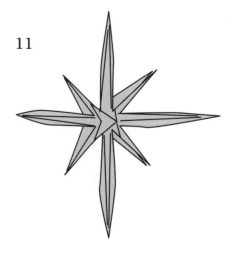

Star

Double Rabbit-Ear

A double rabbit ear is a way to bend and thin a triangular flap. It is often used for making legs. This is much easier than it looks. Once the fold shown in step 5 is started at the top point, the rest of the folding follows naturally.

Double Rabbit-Ear Practice Model

1
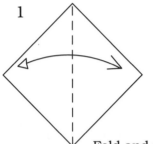
Fold and unfold.

2
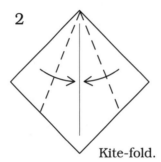
Kite-fold.

3

Kite-fold.

4

This shape is called the Diamond Base.

5
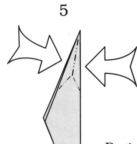
Begin the double rabbit-ear by folding the front and back of the top in half,

6
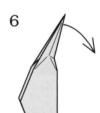
A three-dimensional intermediate step, fold the top in half to one side.

7
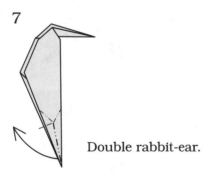
Double rabbit-ear.

8

Review

Here is a list of types of folds and different structures and bases. A few models will be shown, each featuring a different type of fold.

Structures and Bases

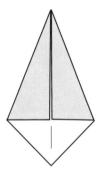

Kite Fold

Diamond Base

Fish Base

Preliminary Fold

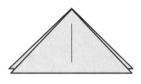

Waterbomb Base

Blintz Fold

Bird Base

Frog Base

Types of Folds

Valley fold
Mountain fold
Unfold
Fold and unfold
Pull out
Squash fold
Petal fold

Minor miracle
Reverse fold
Outside reverse fold
Crimp fold
Sink
Rabbit ear
Double rabbit ear

Car

Fold this model to practice making
squash folds; ten squash folds are used.

1

Fold and unfold.

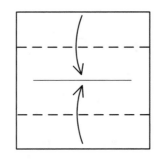

2

Fold to the center.

3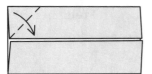

Fold a corner
towards the center.

4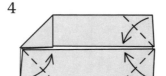

Fold the other corners
towards the center.

5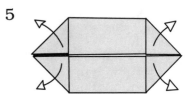

Unfold.

6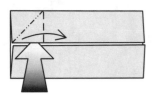

Squash-fold.

7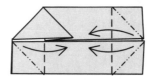

Three more
squash folds.

8

9

Fold close to the end.

10

Bring the right dot to the left
one, which is a bit beyond
the edge of the paper.

11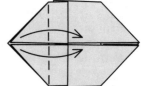

12

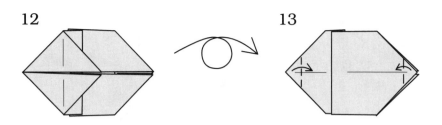

13

14

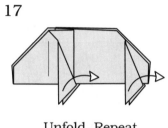

15

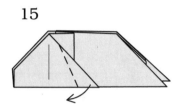

16

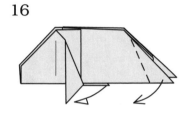

Fold the other
three wheels.

17

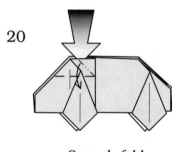

Unfold. Repeat
behind.

18

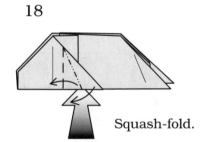

Squash-fold.

19

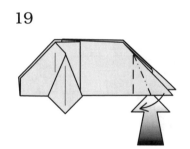

Squash-fold the
other three wheels.

20

Squash-fold.
Repeat behind.

21

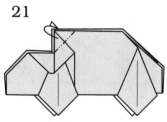

Fold behind.
Repeat behind.

22

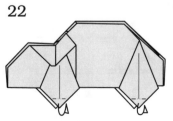

Repeat behind.

23

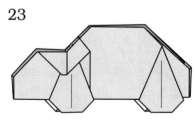

Car

Fish

This model uses many reverse
folds. The dotted line in step 16
is used for an x-ray view.

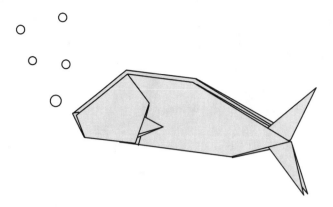

1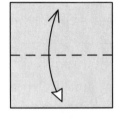

Fold and unfold.

2

Fold to the center.

3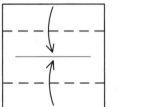

Fold a corner
towards the center.

4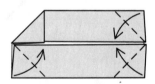

Fold the other corners
towards the center.

5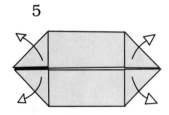

Unfold.

6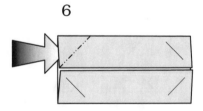

Reverse-fold.

7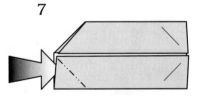

Reverse-fold.

8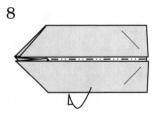

9

Fold the dot to the bottom
line. Repeat behind.

10

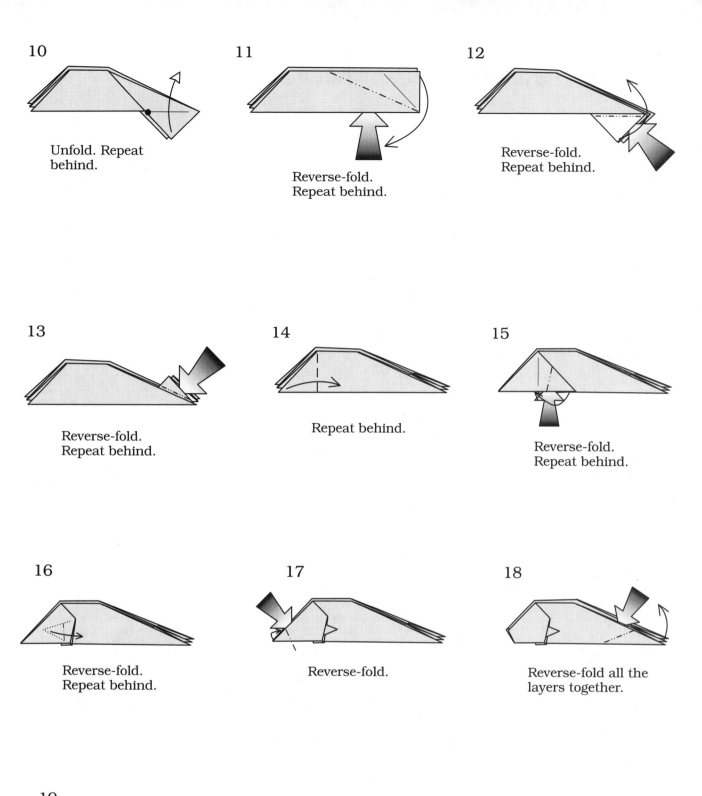

Unfold. Repeat
behind.

11

Reverse-fold.
Repeat behind.

12

Reverse-fold.
Repeat behind.

13

Reverse-fold.
Repeat behind.

14

Repeat behind.

15

Reverse-fold.
Repeat behind.

16

Reverse-fold.
Repeat behind.

17

Reverse-fold.

18

Reverse-fold all the
layers together.

19

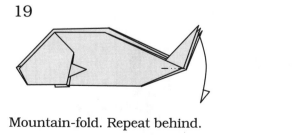

Mountain-fold. Repeat behind.

20

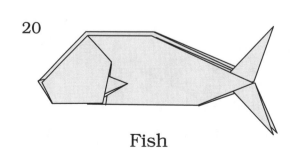

Fish

Three-Headed Moat Monster

This model uses the bird base along
with several outside reverse folds.

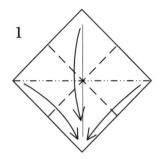

1

Make the
preliminary fold.

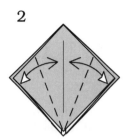

2

Fold and unfold.
Repeat behind.

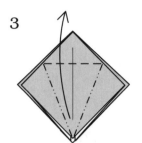

3

Petal-fold.

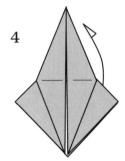

4

Petal-fold behind.

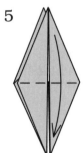

5

Do not repeat
behind.

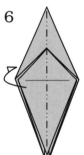

6

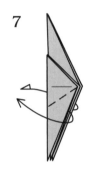

7

Outside-reverse-fold.

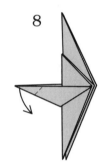

8

Outside-reverse-fold.

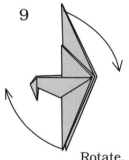

9

Rotate.

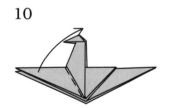

10

Fold up. Repeat
behind.

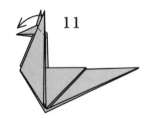

11

Outside-reverse-fold.
Repeat behind.

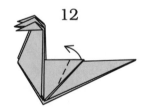

12

Outside-reverse-fold.

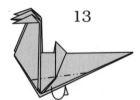

13

Fold inside. Repeat behind.

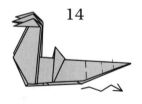

14

Fold the tail
back and forth.

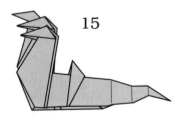

15

Moat Monster

Goose

This model uses the bird base along with several double rabbit ear folds.

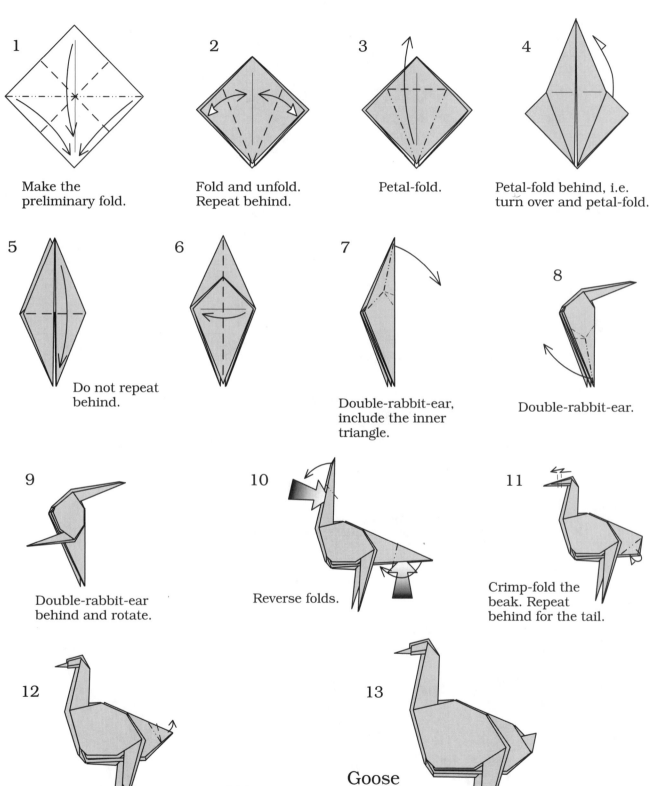

1 Make the preliminary fold.

2 Fold and unfold. Repeat behind.

3 Petal-fold.

4 Petal-fold behind, i.e. turn over and petal-fold.

5 Do not repeat behind.

6

7 Double-rabbit-ear, include the inner triangle.

8 Double-rabbit-ear.

9 Double-rabbit-ear behind and rotate.

10 Reverse folds.

11 Crimp-fold the beak. Repeat behind for the tail.

12 Crimp folds. Repeat behind.

13 Goose

Chapter 2—Intermediate

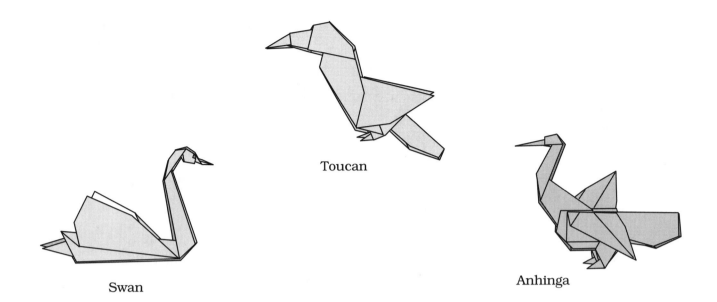

Toucan

Swan

Anhinga

These models, all original, build upon the basic folds shown in chapter 1.

The Swan uses several reverse folds, the Toucan is from the fish base, the Anhinga from the bird base. Then comes the five and six-sided squares for the Lily and Crane. The blintz bird base is used for the Canary and the Dragon is from the stretched bird base.

Mammals are very interesting to fold. The Pig, Cat, and Boar use similar techniques. The Lion and Camel use some molding to make them three dimensional. Being able to fold these high intermediate models shows good progress.

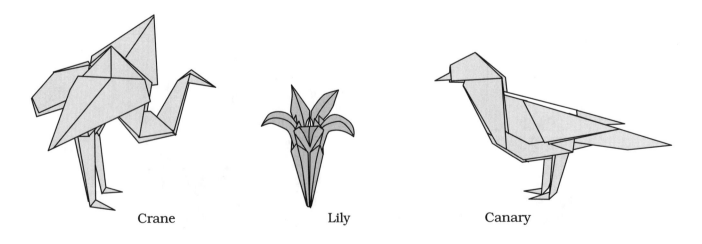

Crane

Lily

Canary

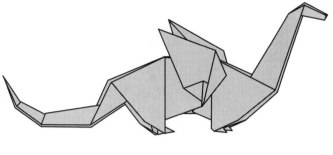

Dragon

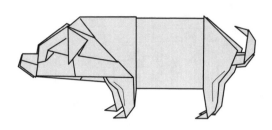

Pig

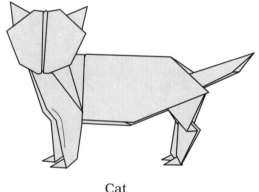

Cat

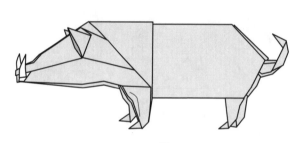

Boar

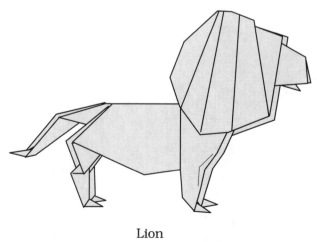

Lion

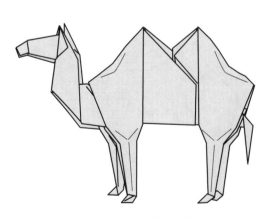

Camel

Swan

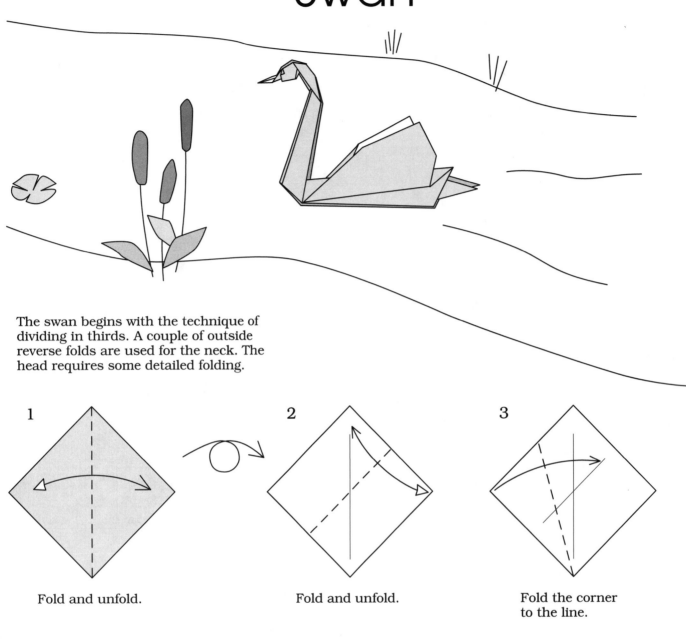

The swan begins with the technique of dividing in thirds. A couple of outside reverse folds are used for the neck. The head requires some detailed folding.

1

Fold and unfold.

2

Fold and unfold.

3

Fold the corner to the line.

4

5

6

7

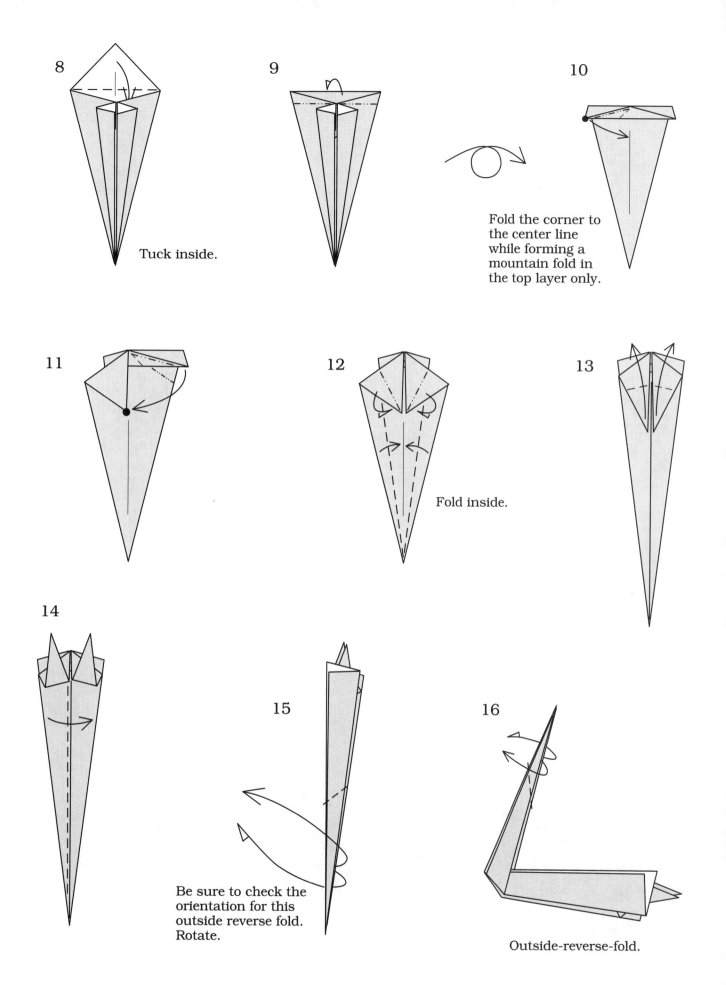

8

Tuck inside.

9

10

Fold the corner to
the center line
while forming a
mountain fold in
the top layer only.

11

12

Fold inside.

13

14

15

Be sure to check the
orientation for this
outside reverse fold.
Rotate.

16

Outside-reverse-fold.

Swan 55

17

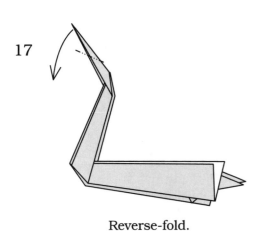

Reverse-fold.

18

Only the head is shown. Fold one of the two layers down to widen the head. Repeat behind.

19

Crimp-fold the beak, folding a few layers together.

20

Fold down to form an eye. Repeat behind.

21

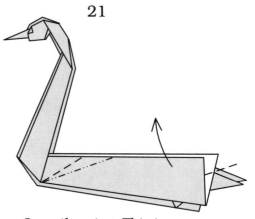

Open the wing. This is similar to a squash fold. Repeat behind.

22

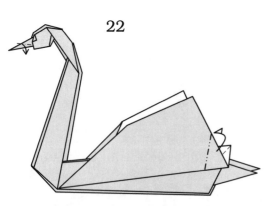

Flatten the beak. Fold inside at the tail. Repeat behind.

23

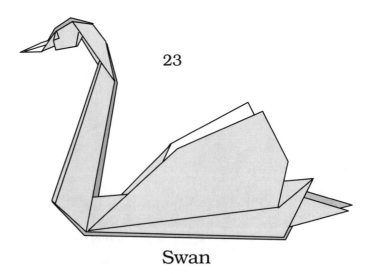

Swan

Toucan

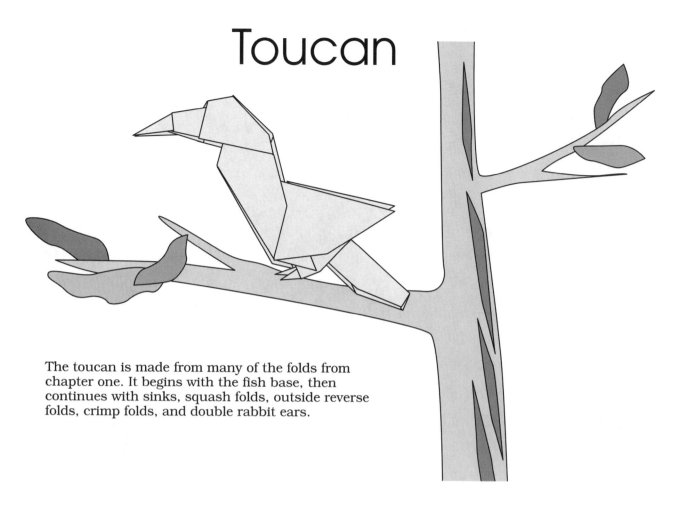

The toucan is made from many of the folds from chapter one. It begins with the fish base, then continues with sinks, squash folds, outside reverse folds, crimp folds, and double rabbit ears.

1

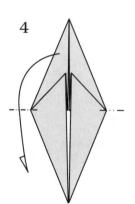

Fold and unfold.

2

Rabbit-ear.

3

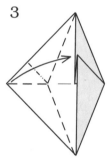

Rabbit-ear.

4

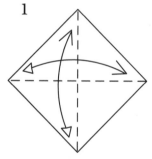

5

This is the fish base.

6

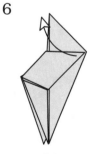

Unfold.

7

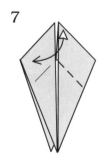

Fold and unfold.

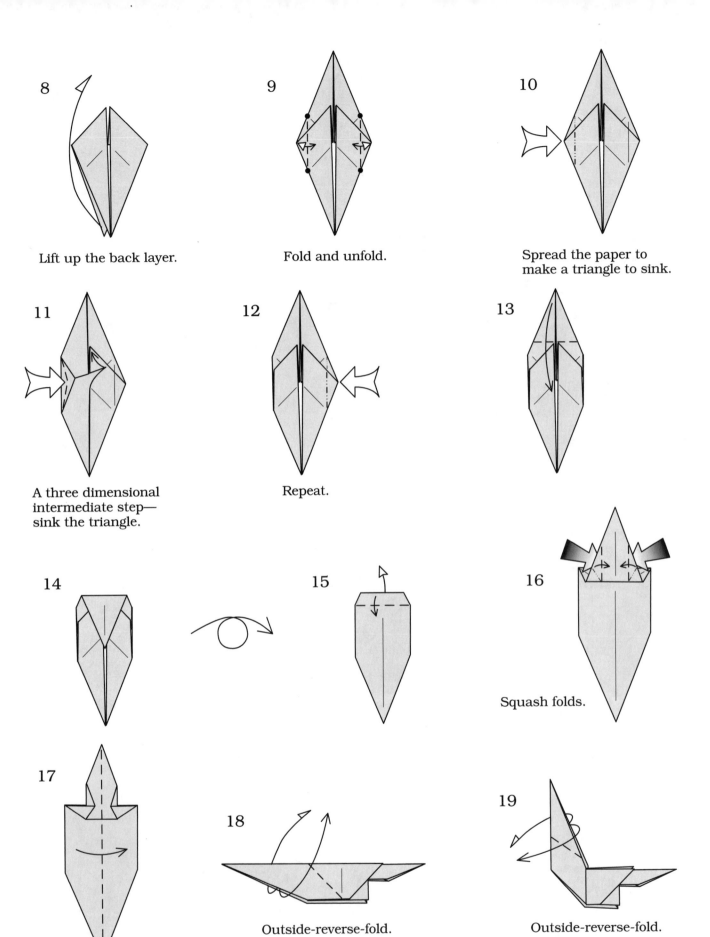

8

Lift up the back layer.

9

Fold and unfold.

10

Spread the paper to make a triangle to sink.

11

A three dimensional intermediate step— sink the triangle.

12

Repeat.

13

14

15

16

Squash folds.

17

18

Outside-reverse-fold.

19

Outside-reverse-fold.

20

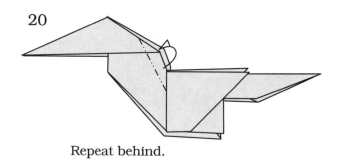

Repeat behind.

21

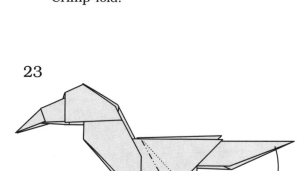

Crimp-fold.

22

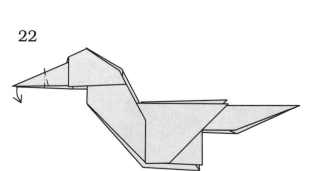

Crimp-fold.

23

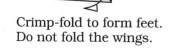

Crimp-fold to form feet.
Do not fold the wings.

24

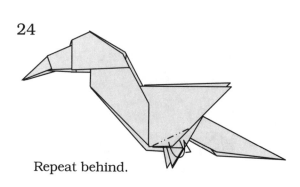

Repeat behind.

25

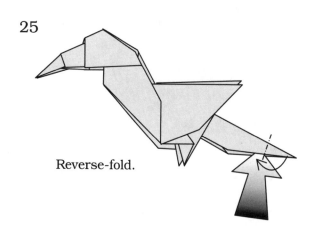

Reverse-fold.

26

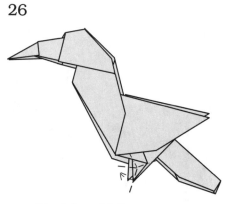

Double-rabbit-ear.
Repeat behind.

27

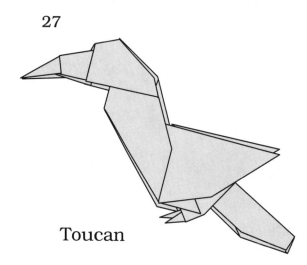

Toucan

Anhinga

The anhinga begins with a bird base with a sink in the center. The four corners of the square become the head, tail, and wings, and the feet are formed from the center.

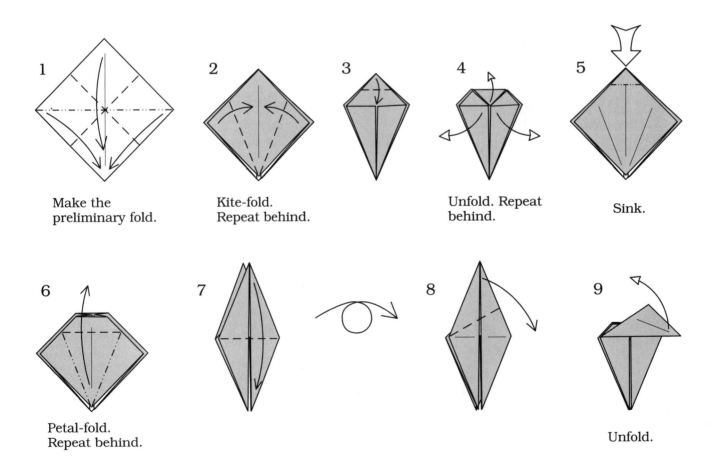

1 Make the preliminary fold.

2 Kite-fold. Repeat behind.

3

4 Unfold. Repeat behind.

5 Sink.

6 Petal-fold. Repeat behind.

7

8

9 Unfold.

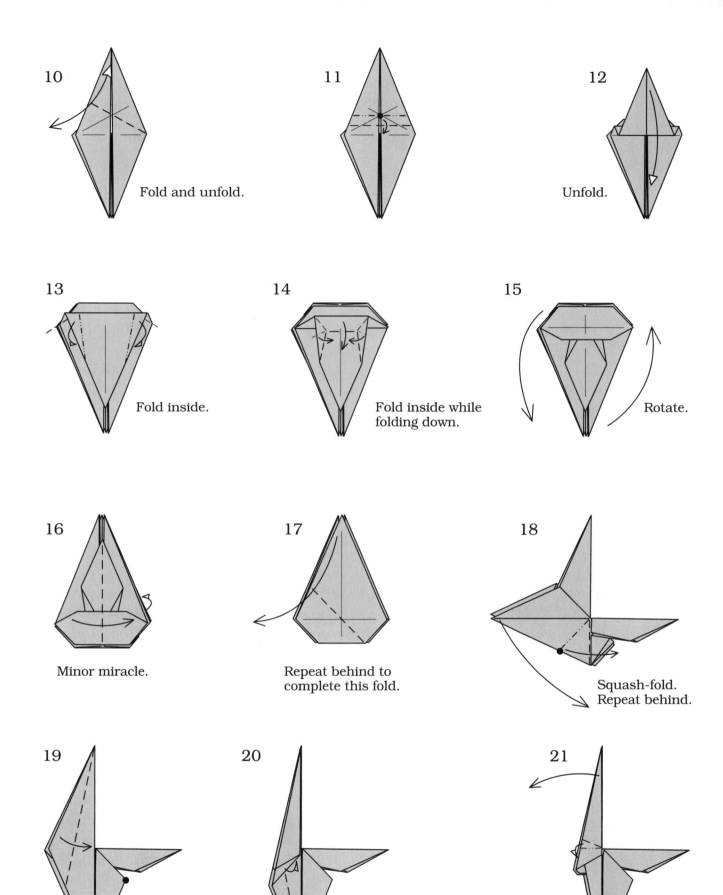

10
Fold and unfold.

11

12
Unfold.

13
Fold inside.

14
Fold inside while folding down.

15
Rotate.

16
Minor miracle.

17
Repeat behind to complete this fold.

18
Squash-fold.
Repeat behind.

19
Repeat behind.

20
Push up and inside at the top.
Repeat behind.

21
Crimp-fold.

Anhinga 61

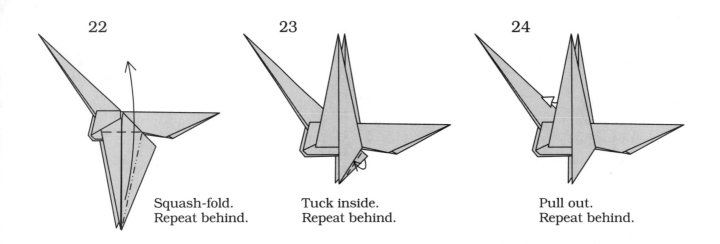

22

Squash-fold.
Repeat behind.

23

Tuck inside.
Repeat behind.

24

Pull out.
Repeat behind.

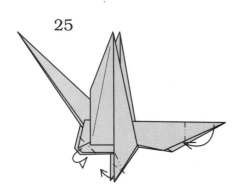

25

Mountain-fold below the
neck, crimp-fold the feet,
and reverse-fold the tail.
Repeat behind.

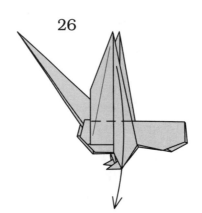

26

Repeat behind.

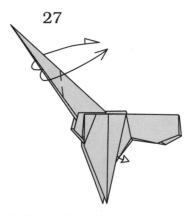

27

Pull out the wings, repeat
behind, and outside-reverse-
fold the neck.

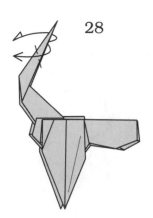

28

Outside-reverse-fold.

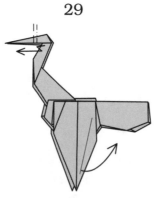

29

Crimp-fold the beak,
and lift the wings.

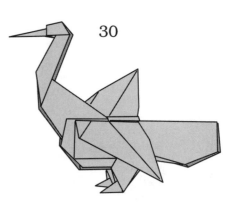

30

Anhinga

Lily

This lily is a variation of the traditional lily. I developed the five-sided square as a way to form five corners instead of the usual four. In two dimensions it looks like a square with extra paper, but in three dimensions you can see how it is composed of five smaller squares connected at the sides. For this model, the preliminary fold is formed with an extra side. A new fold, the spread-squash fold, will be used (step 18).

1

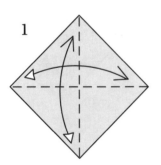

Fold and unfold.

2

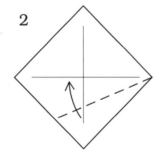

Crease lightly.

3

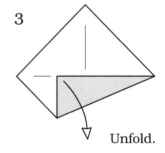

Unfold.

4

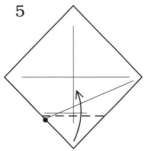

Fold up to the center and unfold. Crease lightly and only on the left side.

5

Fold up so the dot meets the line above it.

6

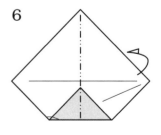

7

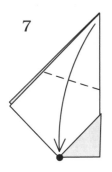

8

Unfold.

9

Reverse-fold.

10

Repeat behind.

11

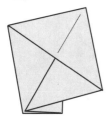

12

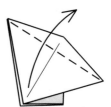

13

14

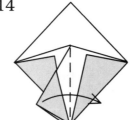

15

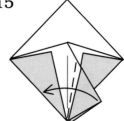

16

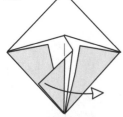

Unfold.

17

Reverse-fold.

18

Spread-squash-fold.

19

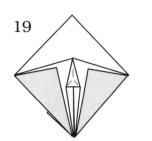

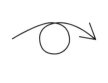

20

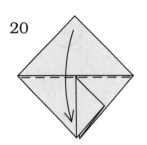

This is the five-sided square.

21

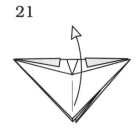

Unfold.

22

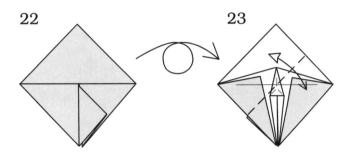

23

Fold and unfold.

24

Fold and unfold.

25

This is similar to the preliminary fold.

26

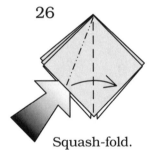

Squash-fold.

27

Squash-fold all the sides.

28

Fold inside.

29

Fold inside on all the sides.

30

31

Thin.

32

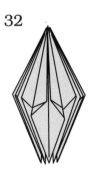

Thin on all the sides.

33

Rotate.

34

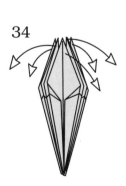

Curl the petals.

35

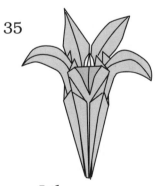

Lily

Crane

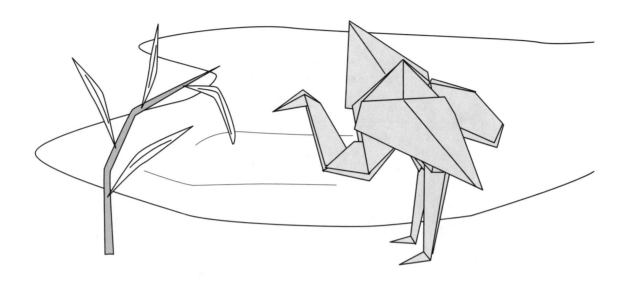

This crane is a variation of the traditional crane. I developed the six-sided square as a way to form six corners instead of the usual four. In two dimensions it looks like a square with extra paper, but in three dimensions you can see how it is composed of six smaller squares connected at the sides. For this model, the preliminary fold and bird base are formed with two more sides.

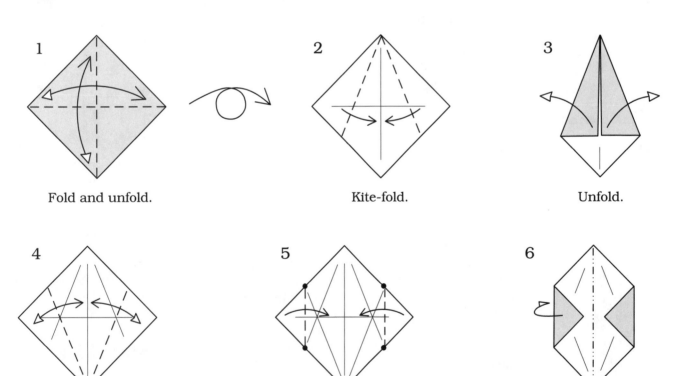

1

Fold and unfold.

2

Kite-fold.

3

Unfold.

4

Fold and unfold.

5

6

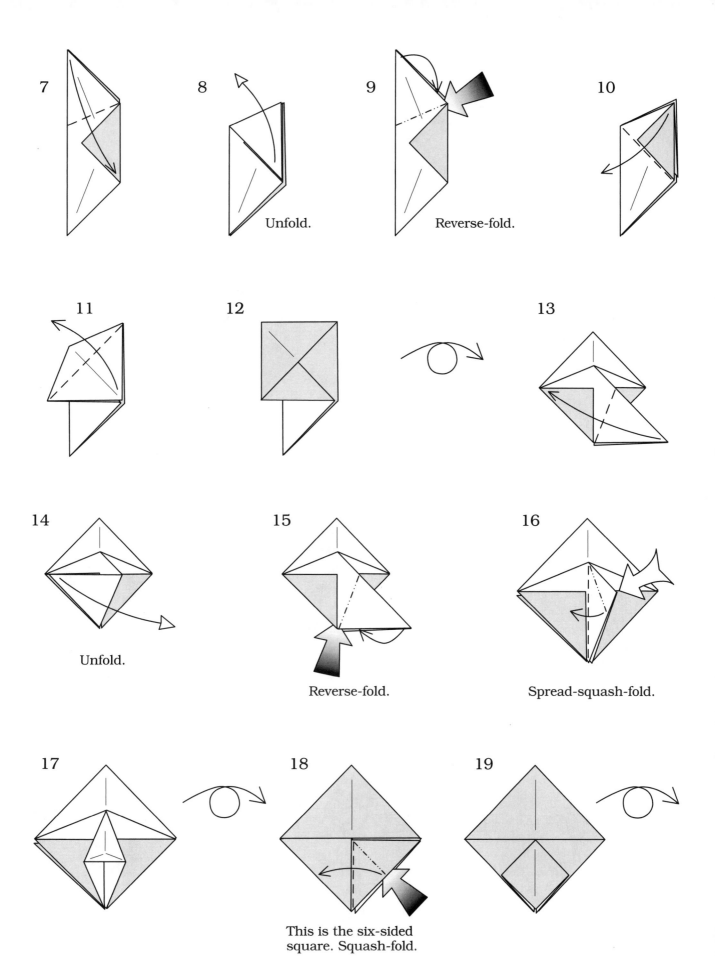

7

8

Unfold.

9

Reverse-fold.

10

11

12

13

14

Unfold.

15

Reverse-fold.

16

Spread-squash-fold.

17

18

This is the six-sided
square. Squash-fold.

19

Crane 67

20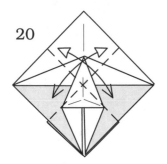

Fold and unfold.

21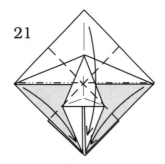

This is the same as
the preliminary fold.

22

23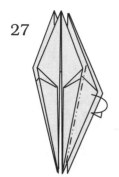

Petal-fold.

24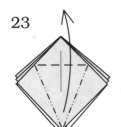

25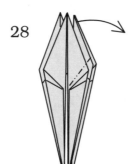

Petal-fold.
Repeat behind.

26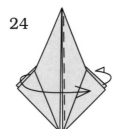

Repeat behind.

27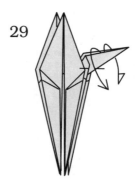

Repeat behind.

28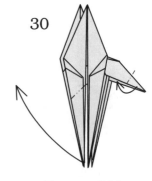

Reverse-fold.

29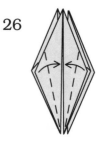

Outside-reverse-fold.

30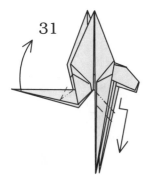

Reverse folds.

31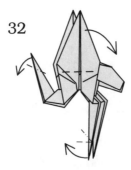

Crimp folds.
Repeat behind.

32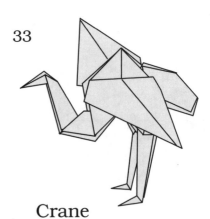

Reverse-fold the head,
crimp-fold the feet, and spread
the wings. Repeat behind.

33

Crane

Canary

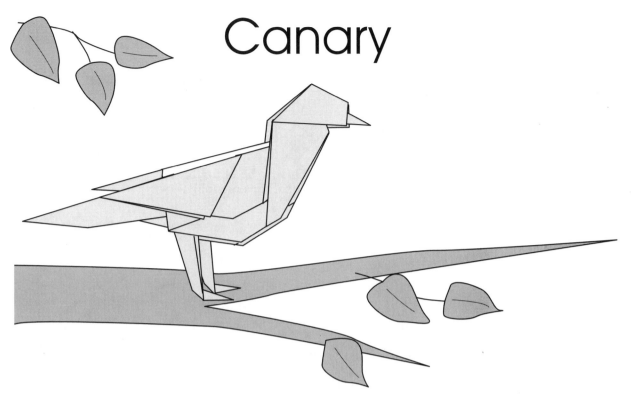

The canary begins with the blintz bird base, and uses spread squashes and reverse folds.

1

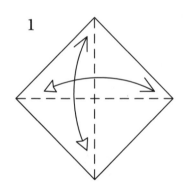

Fold and unfold along the diagonals.

2

Fold the corners to the center.

3

Fold and unfold along the diagonals.

4

Turn over and rotate.

5

This is the same as a preliminary fold.

6

Petal-fold.

7

Pull out the hidden corners.

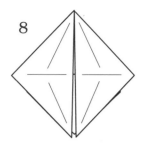

8

Repeat steps
6–7 behind.

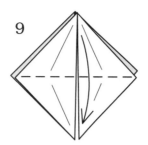

9

Repeat behind.

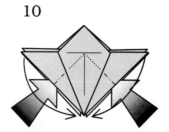

10

This is the blintz bird
base. Reverse folds.

11

Reverse folds.

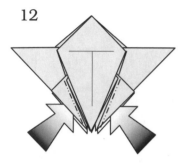

12

Reverse folds.

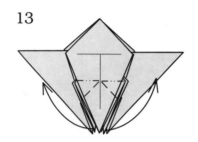

13

Slide the legs up
for this crimp fold.

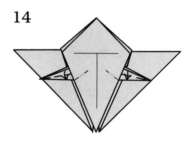

14

Thin the legs.

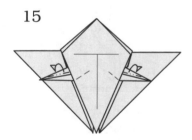

15

Continue thinning
the legs.

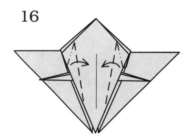

16

Spread squash folds.

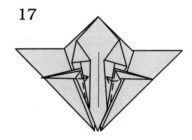

17

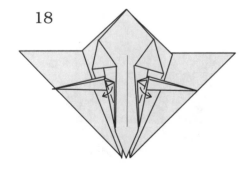

18

19

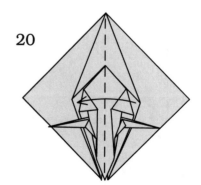

20

21

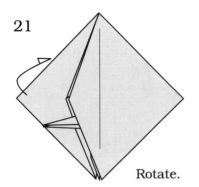

Rotate.

22

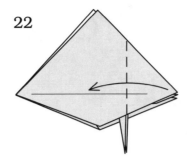

Repeat behind.

23

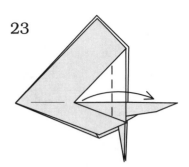

Repeat behind.

24

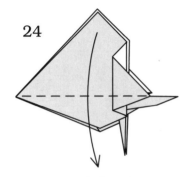

Repeat behind.

25

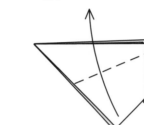

Repeat behind.

26

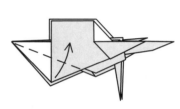

Repeat behind.

27

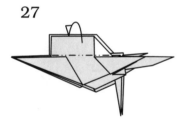

Repeat behind.

28

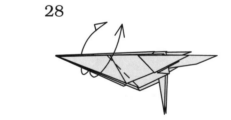

Outside-reverse-fold.

29

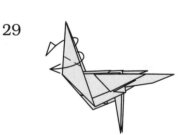

Outside-reverse-fold.

30

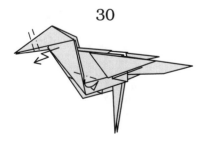

Crimp-fold the beak. Repeat behind for the wings.

31

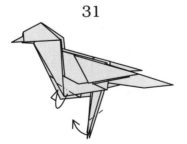

Reverse-fold the feet. Repeat behind.

32

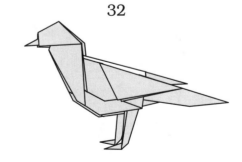

Canary

Dragon

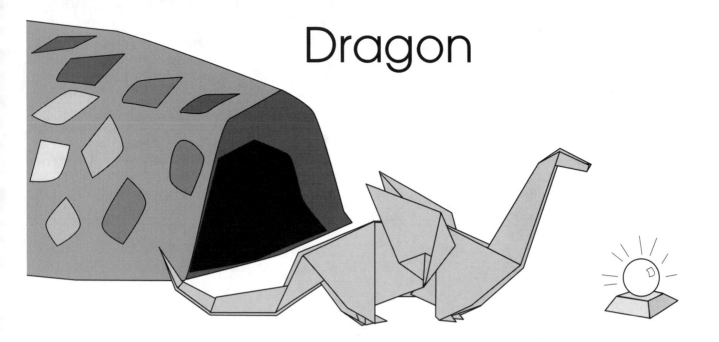

The stretched bird base is used to fold the dragon. After folding the bird base, two opposite corners are pulled apart to stretch the base. The four legs are formed from the center of the paper.

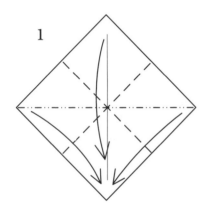

1

Make the preliminary fold.

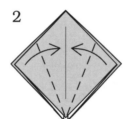

2

Kite-fold. Repeat behind.

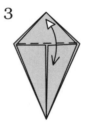

3

Fold and unfold.

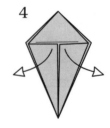

4

Unfold. Repeat behind.

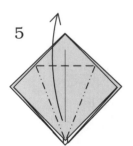

5

Petal-fold.

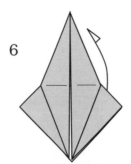

6

Petal-fold behind.

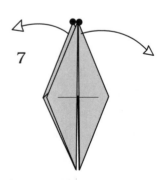

7

Pull the two corners apart as far as possible.

8

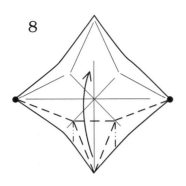

This is three-dimensional.

9

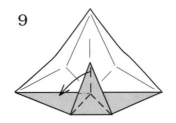

Rabbit-ear.

10

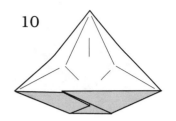

Repeat steps 8–9 on the top half of the model.

11

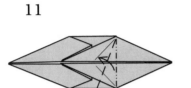

Fold to the crease.

12

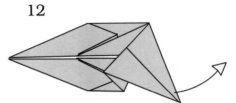

Unfold.

13

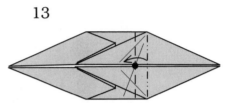

14

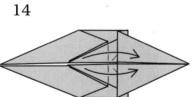

15

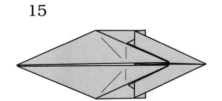

Repeat steps 11–13 on the left.

16

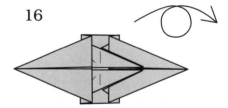

17

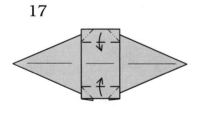

Petal folds.

18

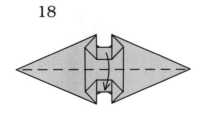

19

Reverse folds.

20

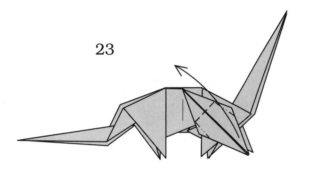

Fold inside.
Repeat behind.

21

Reverse folds.

22

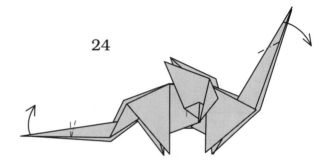

Squash-fold.
Repeat behind.

23

Petal-fold.
Repeat behind.

24

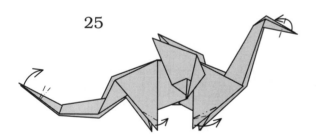

Reverse-fold the head
and crimp-fold the tail.

25

Reverse-fold the head, crimp-fold the
front legs, reverse-fold the back legs,
and crimp-fold the tail. Repeat behind.

26

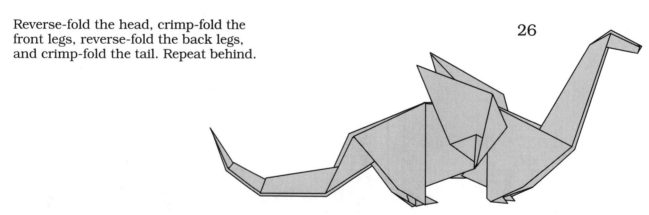

Dragon

Pig

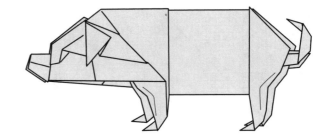

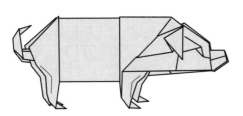

Mammals are among the most difficult of designs to create but luckily they are not so difficult to fold. The pig is formed from a method of folding into a rectangle which makes it possible to form legs in a simple way. It is folded with a seamless closed back, generally considered to be the more realistic and artistic form.

1

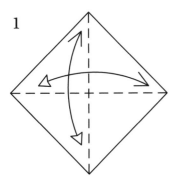

Fold and unfold
along the diagonals.

2

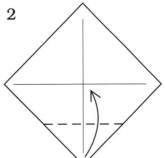

3

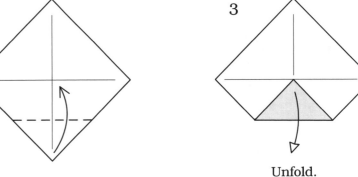

Unfold.

4

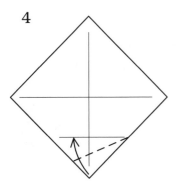

5

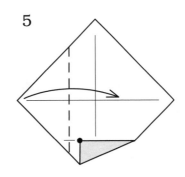

6

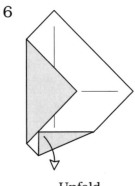

Unfold.

7

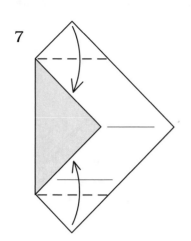

8

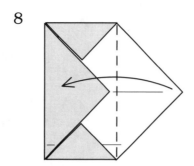

9

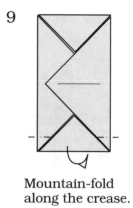

Mountain-fold
along the crease.

10

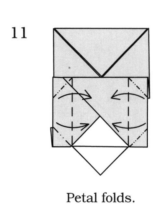

11

Petal folds.

12

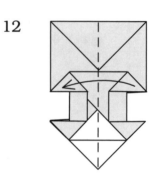

13

Repeat behind.

14

1. Repeat behind.
2. Reverse-fold.

15

1. Squash-fold.
2. Reverse-fold.
Repeat behind.

16

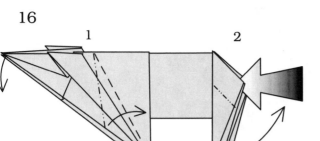

1. Crimp-fold.
2. Reverse-fold.

17

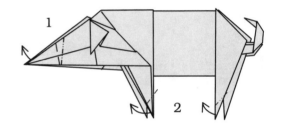

1. Tuck inside.
2. Thin the tail.
Repeat behind.

18

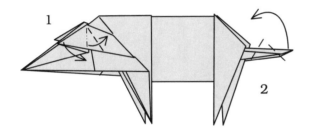

1. Fold the ear down.
   Repeat behind.
2. Outside reverse folds.

19

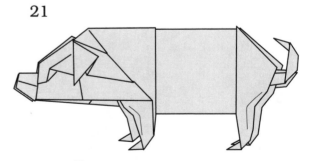

1. Crimp-fold.
2. Reverse folds. Repeat behind.

20

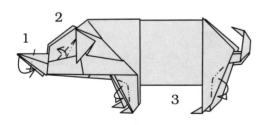

1. Reverse-fold.
2. Lift to form the eye.
3. Shape the legs.
Repeat behind.

21

Pig

Cat

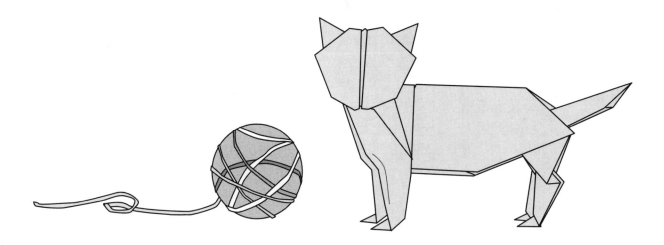

The cat uses another method of folding a rectangle from which we can form legs in a simple way.

1

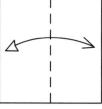

Fold and unfold.

2

Fold to the center.

3

4

5

Unfold.

6

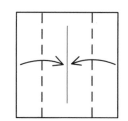

7

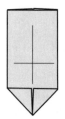

8

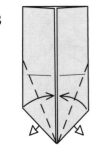

9

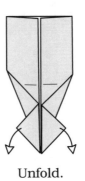

Unfold.

10

Reverse-fold.

11

Reverse-fold.

12

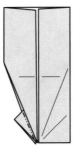

Reverse-fold.

13

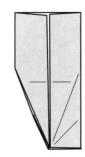

Repeat steps 10–12 on the right.

14

Fold and unfold.

15

Fold and unfold.

16

17

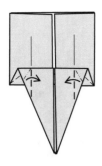

Squash folds.

18

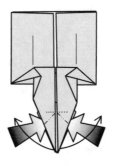

Reverse folds.

19

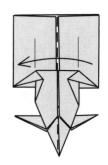

Cat 79

20

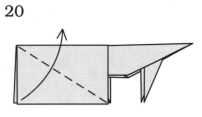

Repeat behind.

21

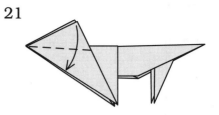

Repeat behind.

22

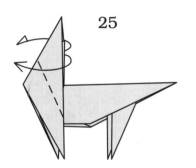

Squash-fold.
Repeat behind.

23

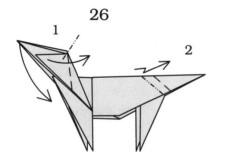

Outside-reverse-fold.

24

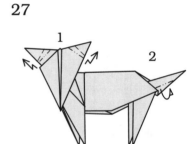

Tuck. Repeat behind.

25

Outside-reverse-fold.

26

1. Squash-fold.
2. Crimp-fold.

27

1. Crimp folds.
2. Repeat behind.

28

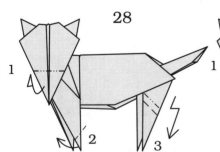

1. Mountain-fold.
2. Reverse-fold.
3. Crimp-fold.
Repeat behind.

29

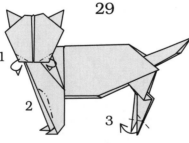

1. Mountain folds.
2. Shape the legs.
3. Crimp-fold.
Repeat behind.

30

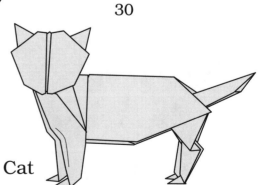

Cat

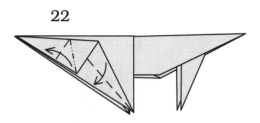
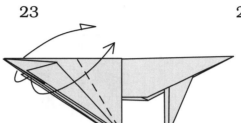
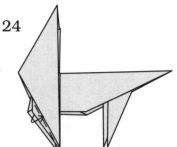

Boar

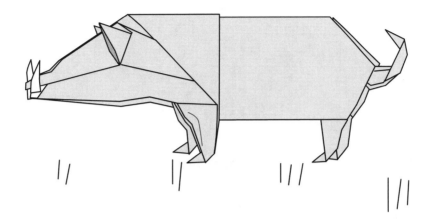

The boar begins in a similar way to the cat.
Two corners become the tusks, then the
folding continues as in the pig.

1

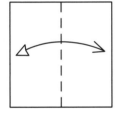

Fold and unfold.

2

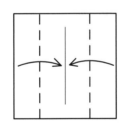

Fold to the center.

3

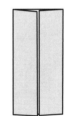

4

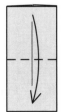

5

Unfold.

6

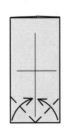

7

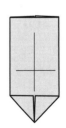

8

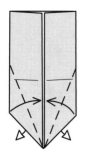

9

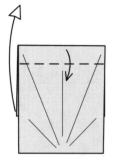

10

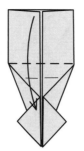

Unfold.

11

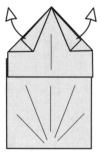

Flip up the back
while folding along
the crease.

12

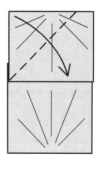

13

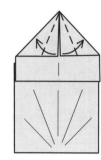

14

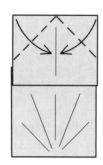

Unfold.

15

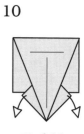

16

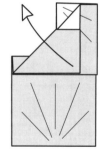

Unfold.

17

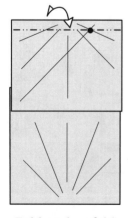

Fold and unfold.

18

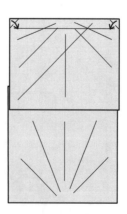

19

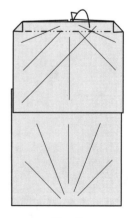

Tuck.

20

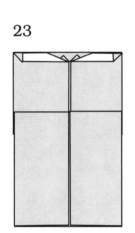

21

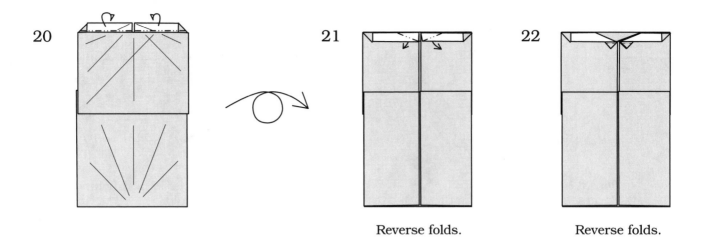

Reverse folds.

22

Reverse folds.

23

Reverse folds.

24

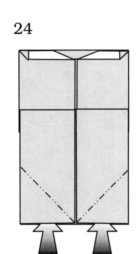

Reverse folds.

25

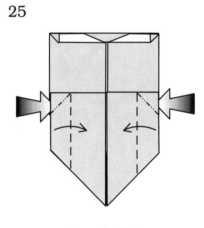

Squash folds.

26

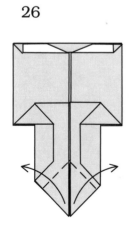

27

28

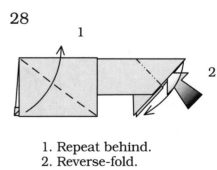

1
2

1. Repeat behind.
2. Reverse-fold.

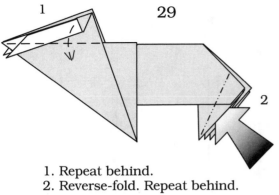

29

1. Repeat behind.
2. Reverse-fold. Repeat behind.

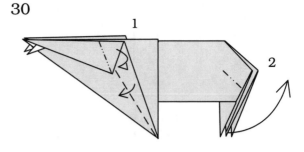

30

1. Fold inside. Repeat behind.
2. Reverse-fold.

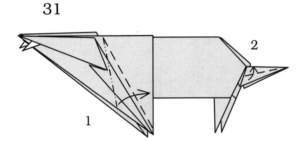

31

1. Crimp-fold.
2. Thin the tail. Repeat behind.

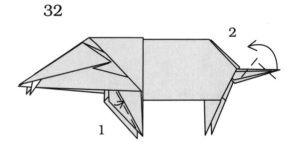

32

1. Tuck, repeat behind.
2. Outside reverse folds.

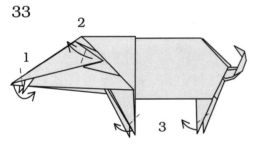

33

1. Reverse-fold.
2. Repeat behind.
3. Reverse folds. Repeat behind.

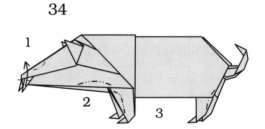

34

Shape the tusks, head, and legs. Repeat behind.

35

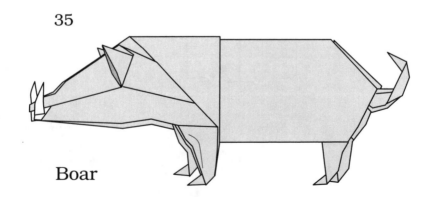

Boar

Lion

The lion uses a technique similar to the cat but with more paper in the front to form the mane.

1

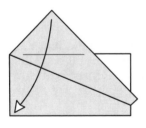

2

Fold and unfold.

3

4

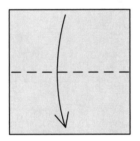

Unfold.

5

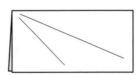

Repeat steps 2–4 on the right and behind.

6

Repeat behind.

7

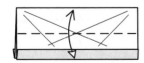

Fold and unfold.
Repeat behind.

8

Fold to the line.
Repeat behind.

9

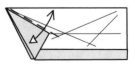

Fold and unfold.
Repeat behind.

10

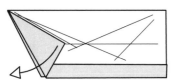

Unfold. Repeat behind.

11

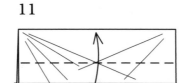

Repeat behind.

12

Fold and unfold.
Repeat behind.

13

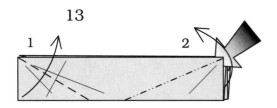

1. Fold along a hidden crease.
2. Reverse-fold.
Repeat behind.

14

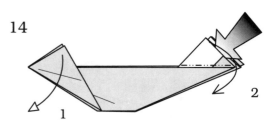

1. Unfold.
2. Reverse-fold.
Repeat behind.

15

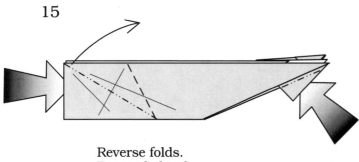

Reverse folds.
Repeat behind.

16

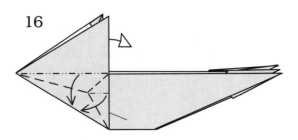

While folding the middle line to the bottom, some paper will be pulled out on the right. Repeat behind.

17

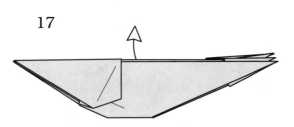

Unfold from behind.

18

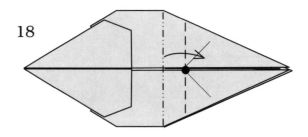

19

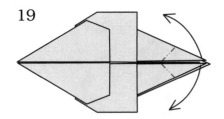

Reverse folds.

20

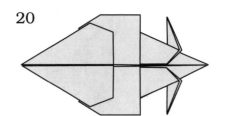

21

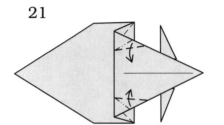

Squash folds.

22

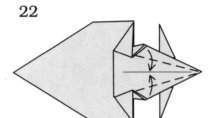

23

Spread-squash folds.

24

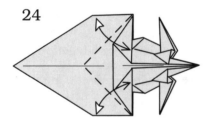

Fold and unfold.

25

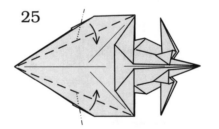

Spread-squash folds.

26

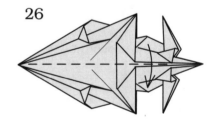

27

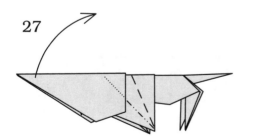

Crimp-fold.

28

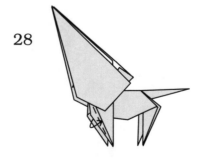

Tuck. Repeat behind.

29

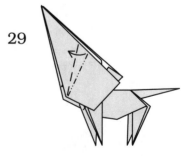

Only fold the top layer.
Repeat behind.

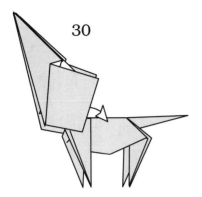

30

Pull out. Repeat behind.

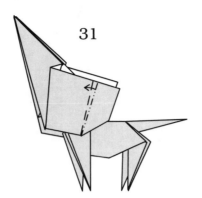

31

Repeat behind.

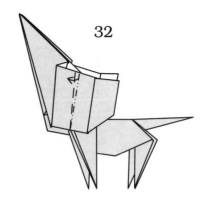

32

Repeat behind.

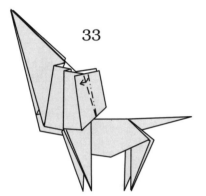

33

Repeat behind.

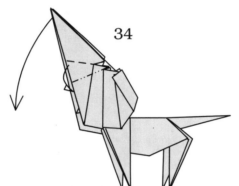

34

Crimp-fold.

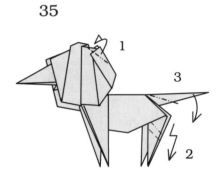

35

1. Fold a few layers together.
   Repeat behind.
2. Reverse folds. Repeat behind.
3. Reverse-fold.

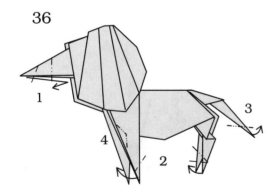

36

1. Reverse folds.
2. Reverse and crimp folds.
3. Reverse-fold.
4. Bend the front legs.
Repeat behind.

37

Lion

Camel

The cat and boar used book-fold symmetry. The camel uses diagonal symmetry. The fold in step 7 gives the camel its proportion (length of body to legs and neck). There is an interesting sequence of folds at steps 23–24 to produce the humps.

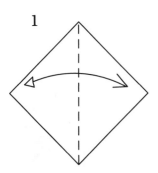

1

Fold and unfold.

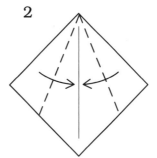

2

Kite-fold.

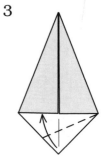

3

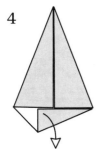

4

Unfold.

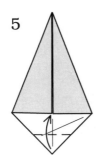

5

6

Unfold.

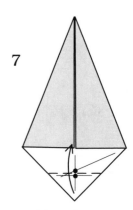

7

Fold up between the dots.

8

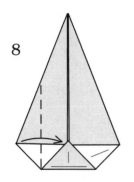

9

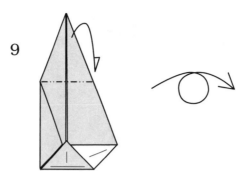

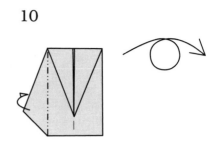

10

11

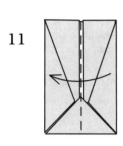

12

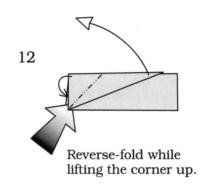

Reverse-fold while
lifting the corner up.

13

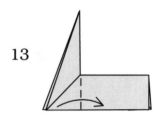

14

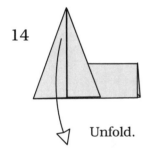

Unfold.

15

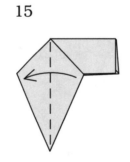

16

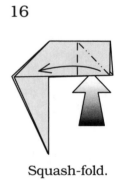

Squash-fold.

17

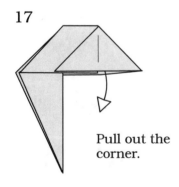

Pull out the
corner.

18

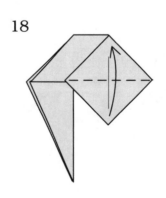

19

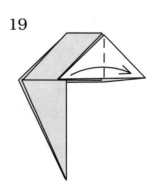

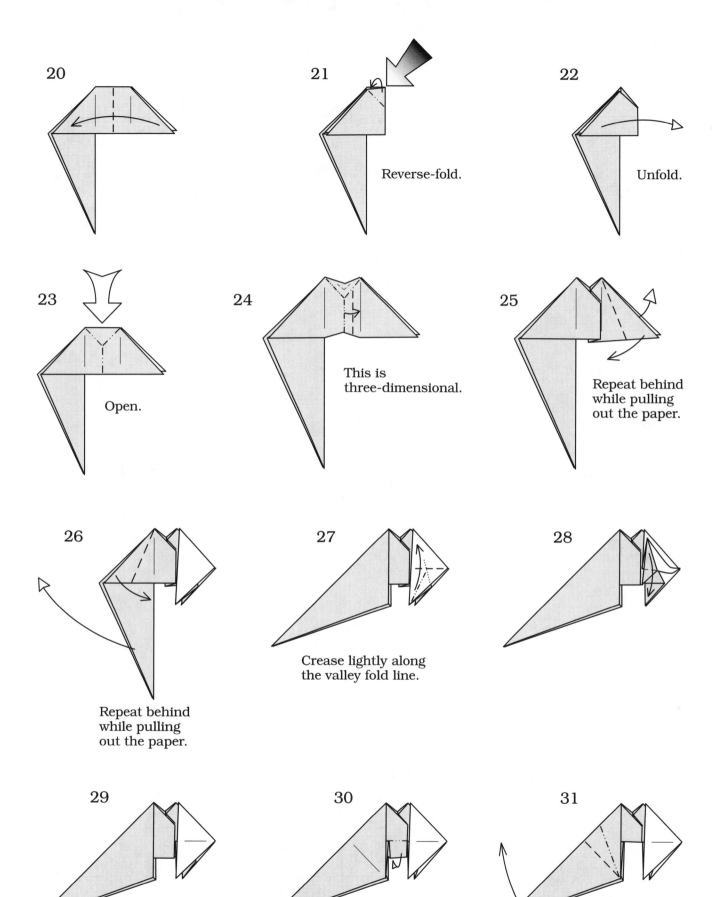

20

21

Reverse-fold.

22

Unfold.

23

Open.

24

This is
three-dimensional.

25

Repeat behind
while pulling
out the paper.

26

Repeat behind
while pulling
out the paper.

27

Crease lightly along
the valley fold line.

28

29

Repeat steps 27–28 on
the three other legs.

30

Repeat behind.

31

Crimp-fold.

Camel 91

32

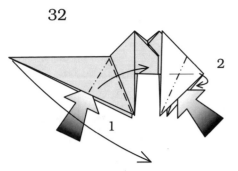

1. Squash-fold.
2. Reverse-fold.

33

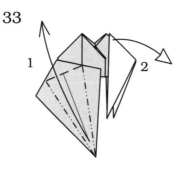

1. Petal-fold.
2. Pull out.

34

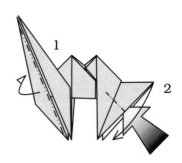

1. Mountain-fold.
2. Reverse-fold.

35

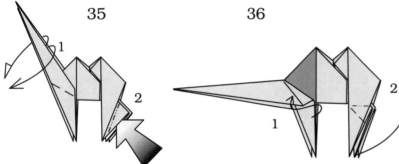

1. Outside-reverse-fold.
2. Reverse-fold. Repeat behind.

36

1. Tuck inside.
   Repeat behind.
2. Crimp-fold.

37

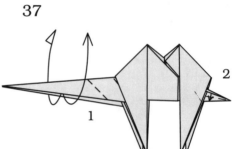

1. Outside-reverse-fold.
2. Thin the tail. Repeat behind.

38

1. Open the head.
2. Outside-reverse-fold.

39

The head is three-dimensional.

40

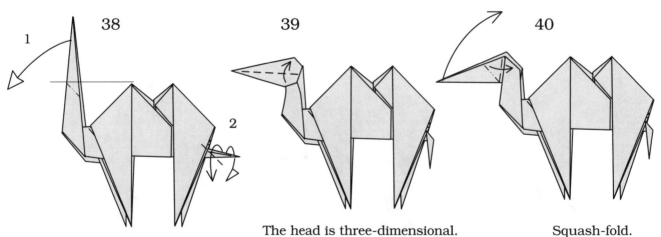

Squash-fold.

41

42

Outside-reverse-fold.

43

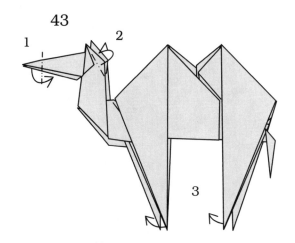

1. Reverse-fold.
2. Repeat behind.
3. Spread to form hooves.
   Repeat behind.

44

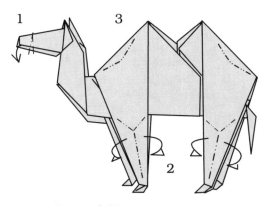

1. Crimp-fold.
2. Thin and shape the legs.
   Repeat behind.
3. Shape the body.

45

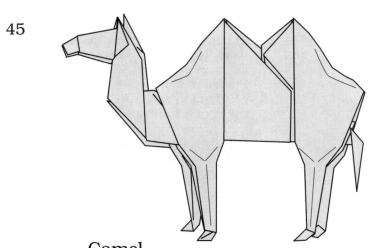

Camel

Chapter 3—Advanced

Fred Rohm's Impossible Vase

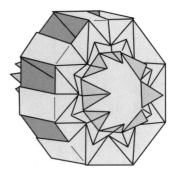

Fred Rohm's Water Wheel

You are now ready to fold advanced models. These have more folds including many difficult steps. Fold slowly and accurately. It might be easier to use larger paper, such as 10 inch squares.

Two of Fred Rohm's models are shown—his Impossible Vase and Water Wheel. They make for very satisfying three dimensional folding. You can tell by the folding methods that there must be many ways to fold these.

Then come some of my models. The Deer is from the waterbomb base. The front legs come from the center of the paper allowing for more paper in the antlers. There is a similarity between the Elephant and the Pig in chapter 2, but we make extra folds in the Elephant to get paper that becomes the tusks. The Bee is from the double blintz bird base to give it all its points.

Being able to fold these advanced models is a sign of mastery with origami.

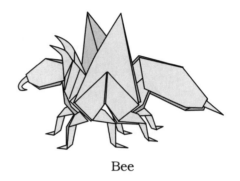

Bee

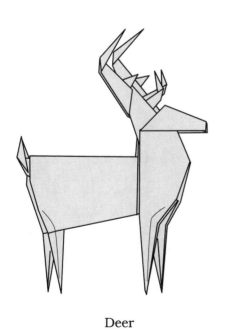

Deer

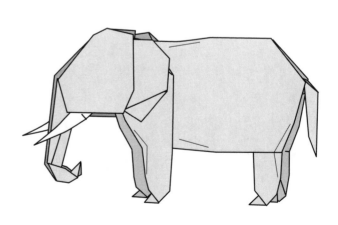

Elephant

Fred Rohm's Impossible Vase

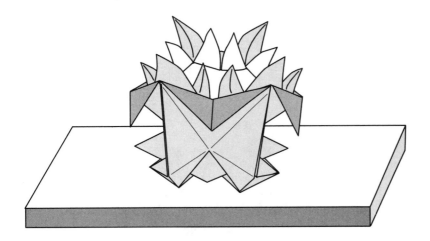

Fred Rohm created this vase as a challenge with folder/creator Neal Elias. The challenge was to come up with as many points as possible. Though not impossible to fold, it was titled the impossible vase because it had more points than previously thought possible.

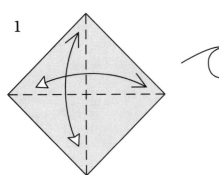

1

Fold and unfold along the diagonals.

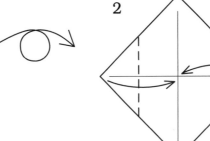

2

Fold two corners to the center.

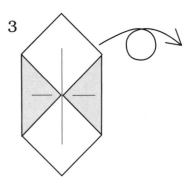

3

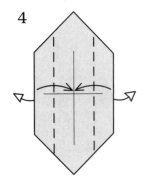

4

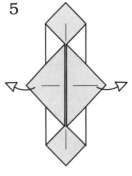

5

Unfold.

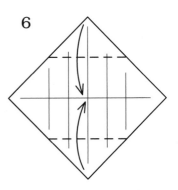

6

Repeat steps 2–5.

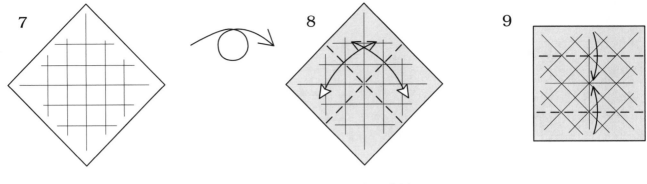

7

8

Fold and unfold.

9

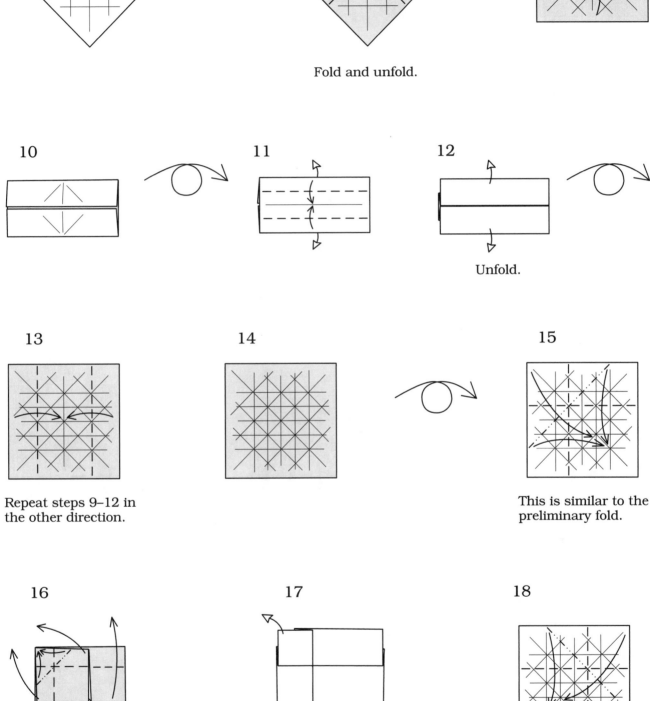

10

11

12

Unfold.

13

Repeat steps 9–12 in the other direction.

14

15

This is similar to the preliminary fold.

16

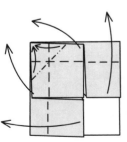

This is also similar to the preliminary fold.

17

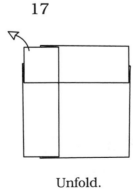

Unfold.

18

Repeat step 15–17 on the three other sides.

19

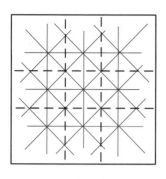

Collapse along
the creases.

20

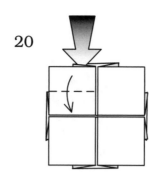

Squash-fold.

21

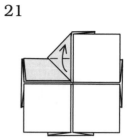

22

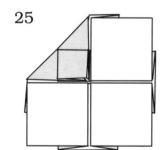

Squash-fold.

23

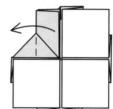

24

This is similar to the
preliminary fold.

25

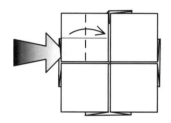

Repeat steps 20–24 on
the three other sides.

26

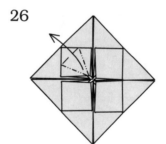

Petal-fold.

27

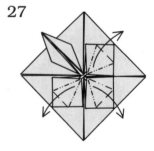

Three more
petal folds.

28

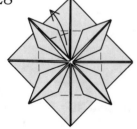

29

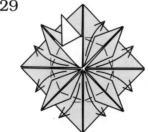

30

31

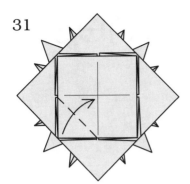

32

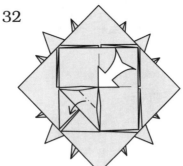

Spread-squash-fold.

33

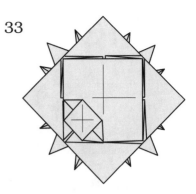

Repeat steps 31–32 on the three other sides.

34

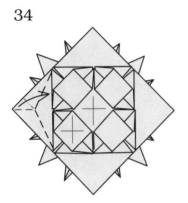

Rabbit-ear.

35

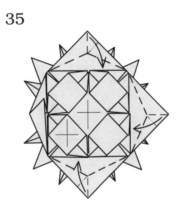

Rabbit-ear on the three other sides.

36

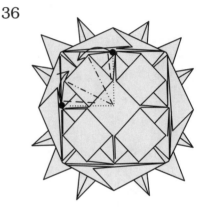

Fold the corners with the dots towards each other. This will become the stand and the model will be three dimensional.

37

This is three dimensional. Continue step 36 on the three other sides.

38

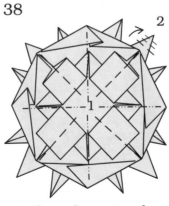

This is three dimensional.
1. Shape the vase so it will stand but keep the base flat.
2. Curl the flaps all around.

39

Fred Rohm's Impossible Vase

Fred Rohm's Water Wheel

Fred Rohm designed this ingenious three dimensional model to be symmetric on the front and back. The folding method shown is just one of several possible ways to obtain the same result.

1

Fold and unfold along the diagonals.

2

Fold the corners to the center.

3

Fold and unfold along the diagonals.

4

5

6

Return to the blintz fold.

7

Repeat steps 5–6.

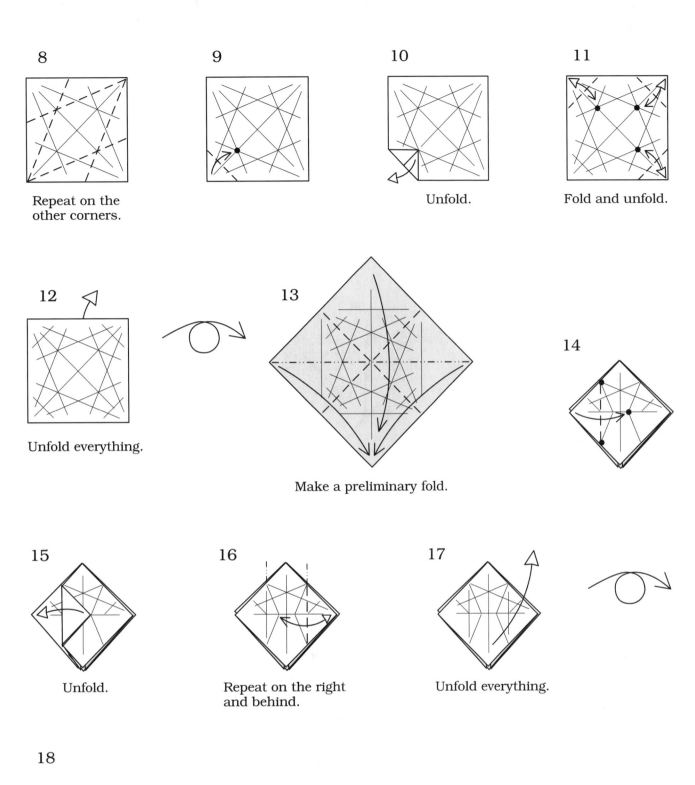

8

Repeat on the
other corners.

9

10

Unfold.

11

Fold and unfold.

12

Unfold everything.

13

Make a preliminary fold.

14

15

Unfold.

16

Repeat on the right
and behind.

17

Unfold everything.

18

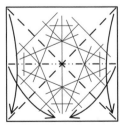

Make a waterbomb
base.

19

Fold and unfold.

20

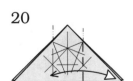

Repeat on the right
and behind.

21

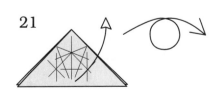

Unfold everything.

22

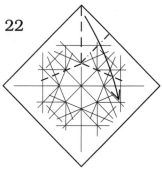

Rabbit-ear.

23

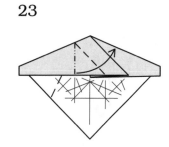

Squash-fold.

24

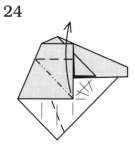

Squash-fold.

25

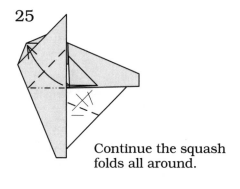

Continue the squash folds all around.

26

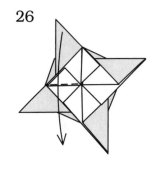

27

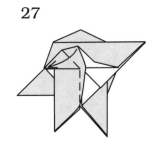

A three-dimensional step.

28

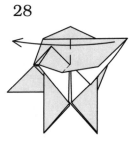

A three-dimensional step.

29

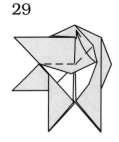

A three-dimensional step. Continue this process all around.

30

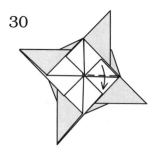

31

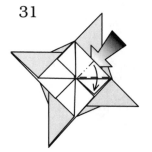

32

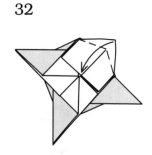

A three-dimensional step.

33

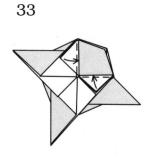

Tuck inside.

34

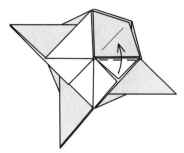

35

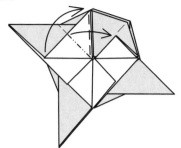

36

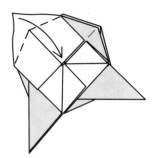

37

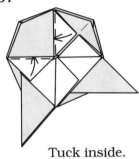

Tuck inside.

38

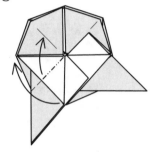

Repeat steps 35–37 on
the two remaining sides.

39

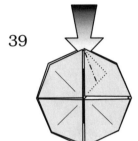

Reverse-fold an
inside layer.

40

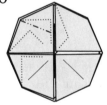

Reverse fold on the
other seven sides.

41

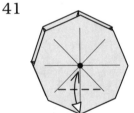

Fold and unfold.

42

Fold and unfold on
the other seven sides.

43

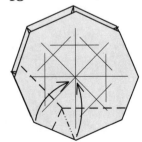

Rabbit-ear.

44

Squash-fold.

45

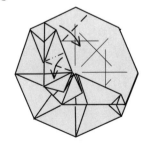

Continue squash-folding
all around.

46

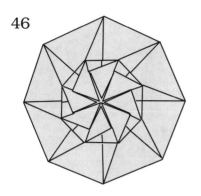

Repeat steps
41–45 behind.

47

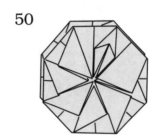

48

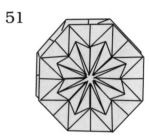

Squash-fold.

49

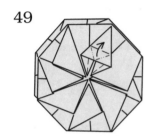

Petal-fold.

50

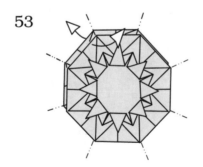

Repeat steps 48–49 on
the seven other sides.

51

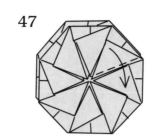

Repeat steps
47–50 behind.

52

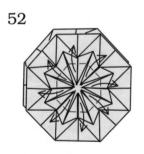

Fold these corners out.
Repeat behind.

53

Separate the front and
back while creasing the
eight middle edges.

54

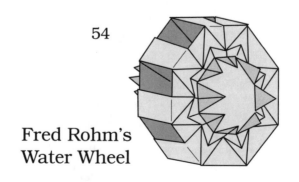

Fred Rohm's
Water Wheel

Deer

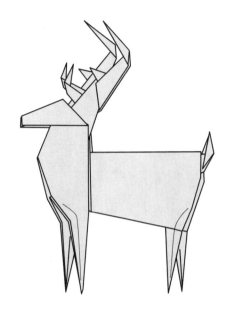

The deer begins with the waterbomb base and a sink. Two corners form the antlers, and the front legs come from the center of the paper.

1

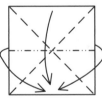

Begin with the waterbomb base.

2

Repeat behind.

3

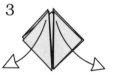

Unfold. Repeat behind.

4

5

Unfold.

6

Repeat steps 4–5 on the right and behind.

7

Fold down and unfold.

8

Sink.

9

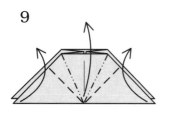

This is similar
to a petal fold.

10

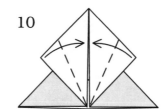

11

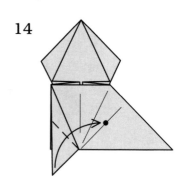

12

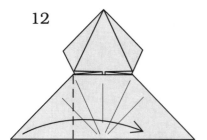

13

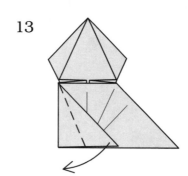

14

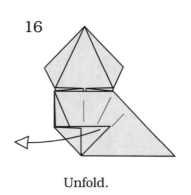

15

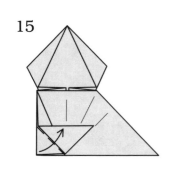

16

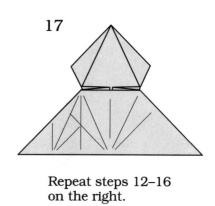

Unfold.

17

Repeat steps 12–16
on the right.

18

Crimp-fold.

19

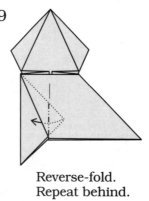

Reverse-fold.
Repeat behind.

20

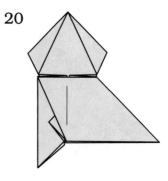

Repeat steps 18–19
on the right.

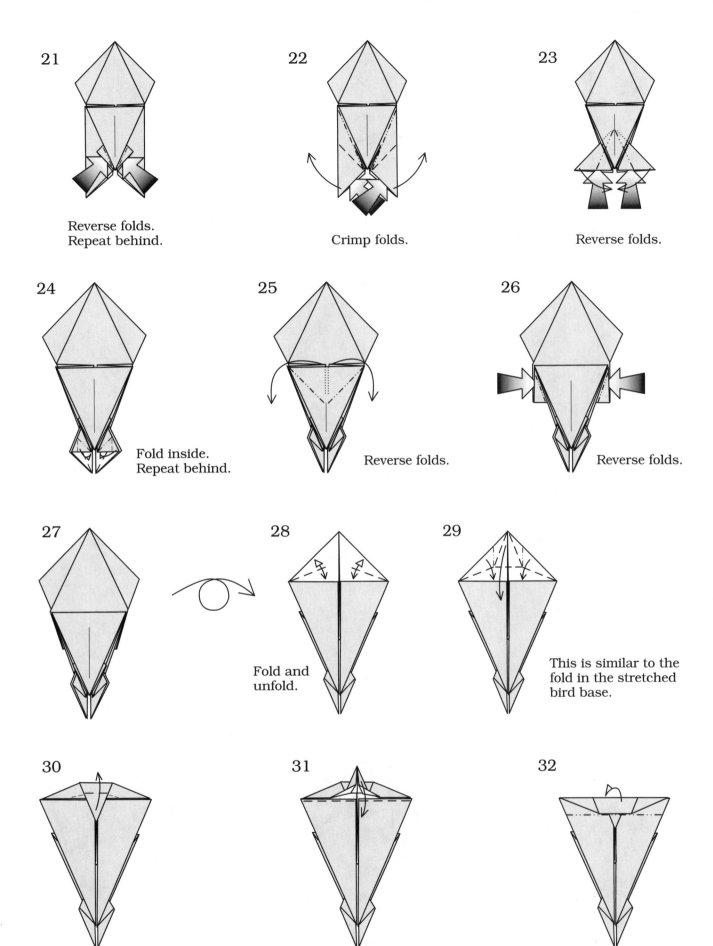

21

Reverse folds.
Repeat behind.

22

Crimp folds.

23

Reverse folds.

24

Fold inside.
Repeat behind.

25

Reverse folds.

26

Reverse folds.

27

28

Fold and
unfold.

29

This is similar to the
fold in the stretched
bird base.

30

31

32

33

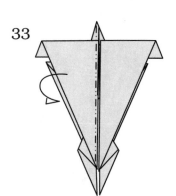

34

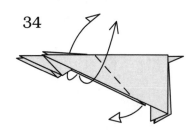

Outside-reverse-fold.

35

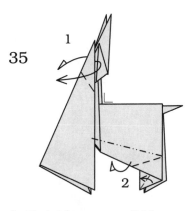

1. Outside-reverse-fold.
2. Fold the legs in half while thinning the body. Repeat behind.

36

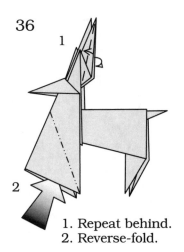

1. Repeat behind.
2. Reverse-fold.

37

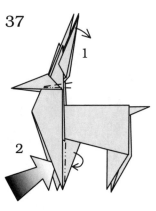

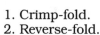

1. Crimp-fold.
2. Reverse-fold.

38

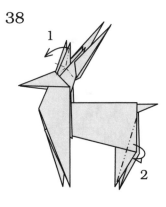

1. Double-rabbit-ear.
2. Tuck inside. Repeat behind.

39

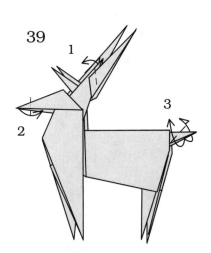

1. Fold only one horn down. Repeat behind.
2. Reverse-fold.
3. Outside-reverse-fold.

40

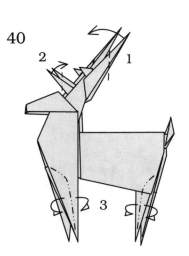

1. Outside-reverse-fold.
2. Reverse-fold.
3. Thin the legs. Repeat behind.

41

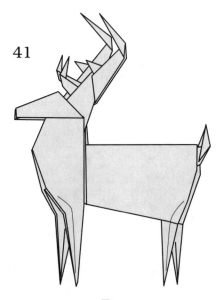

Deer

Elephant

Elephants are fun to fold and fun to create. I have probably created more elephants than any other animal. This model is more challenging than other models in the book because it has white tusks. It uses a stlye similar to the pig.

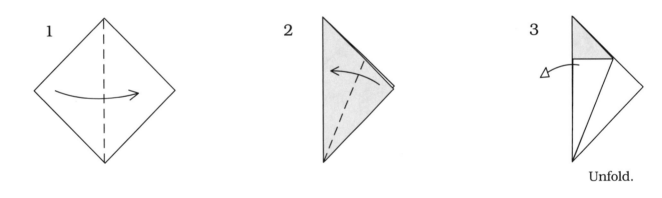

1

2

3

Unfold.

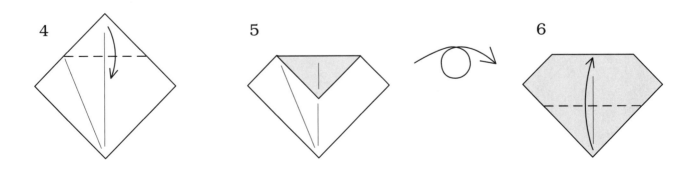

4

5

6

7

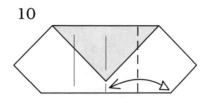

8

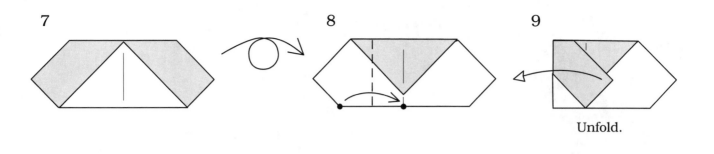

9

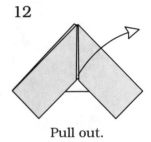

Unfold.

10

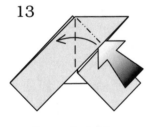

Fold and unfold.

11

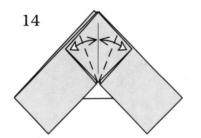

12

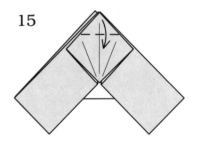

Pull out.

13

Squash-fold.

14

Fold and unfold.

15

16

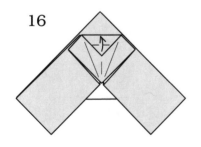

17

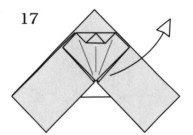

Unfold everything.

18

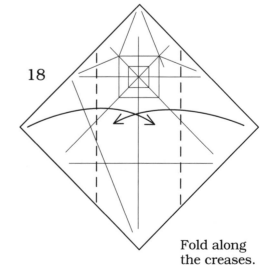

Fold along
the creases.

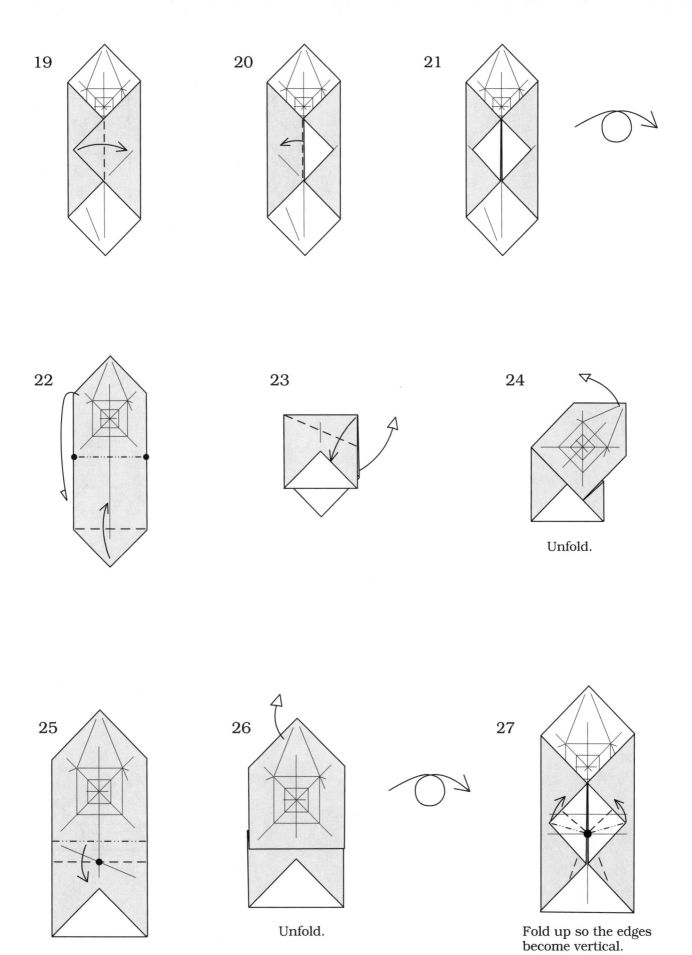

19

20

21

22

23

24

Unfold.

25

26

Unfold.

27

Fold up so the edges
become vertical.

28

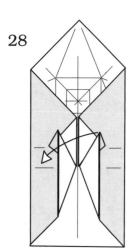

Note the bold,
vertical lines.
Unfold.

29

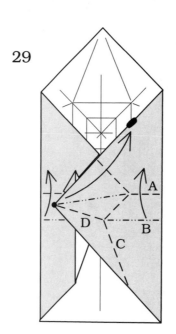

New lines will be formed
by collapsing along the
creases. Lines A, B, C,
and D already exist.

30

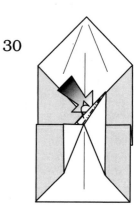

Reverse-fold.

31

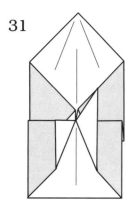

Repeat steps
29–30 on the left.

32

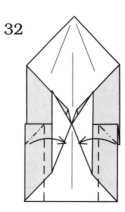

Squash folds.

33

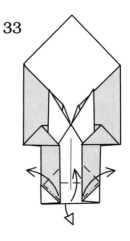

34

35

36

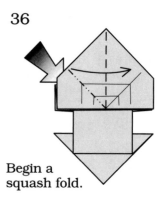

Begin a
squash fold.

37

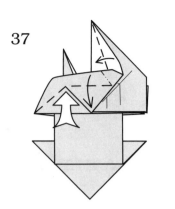

This is a three-dimensional
intermediate step.

38

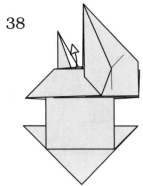

Pull out.

39

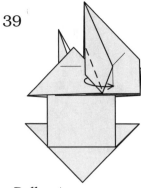

Pull out.

40

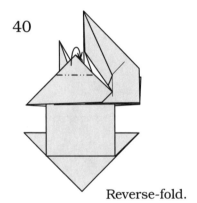

Reverse-fold.

41

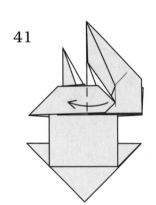

42

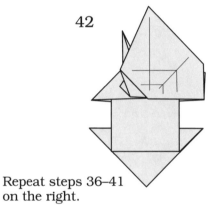

Repeat steps 36–41
on the right.

43

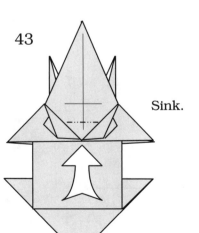

Sink.

44

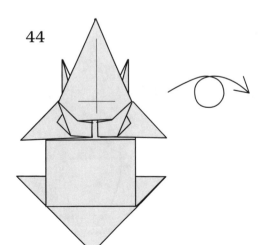

45

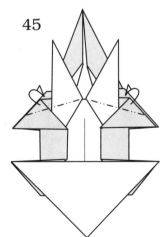

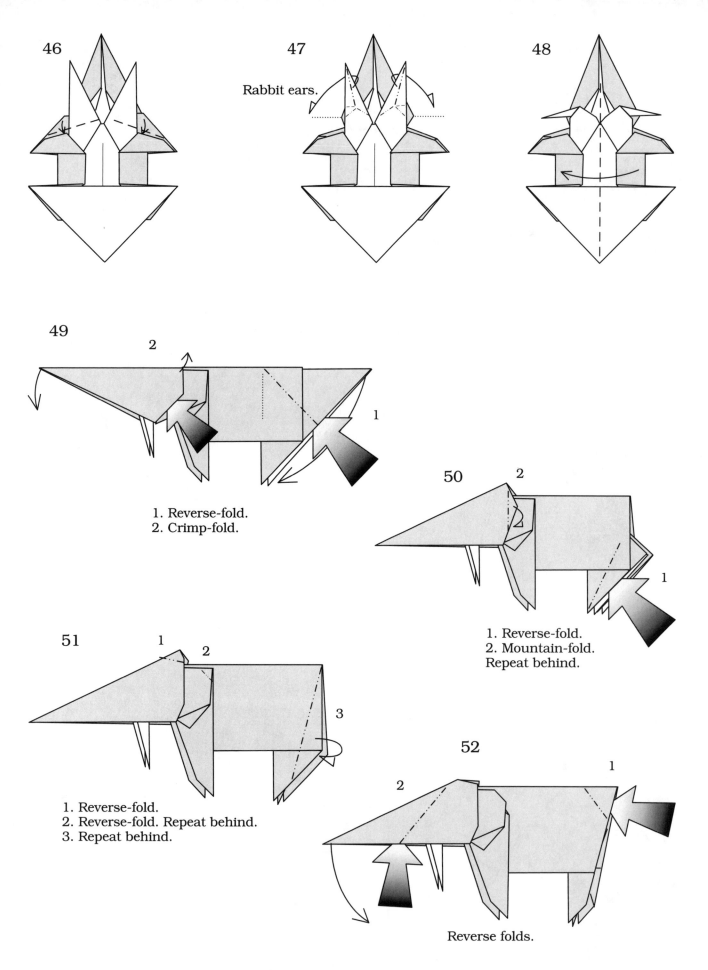

46

47 Rabbit ears.

48

49

1. Reverse-fold.
2. Crimp-fold.

50

1. Reverse-fold.
2. Mountain-fold.
Repeat behind.

51

1. Reverse-fold.
2. Reverse-fold. Repeat behind.
3. Repeat behind.

52

Reverse folds.

53

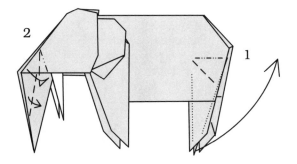

1. Crimp-fold.
2. Thin the trunk.
   Repeat behind.

54

1. Reverse-fold.
2. Crimp-fold.
3. Reverse and crimp folds.
Repeat behind.

55

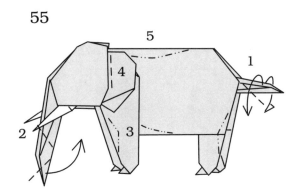

Outside-reverse-fold the
tail, reverse-fold the trunk,
and shape the legs, ears,
and back. Repeat behind.

56

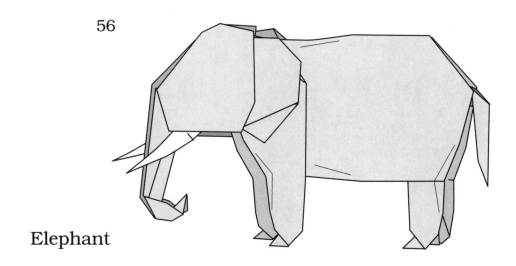

Elephant

Bee

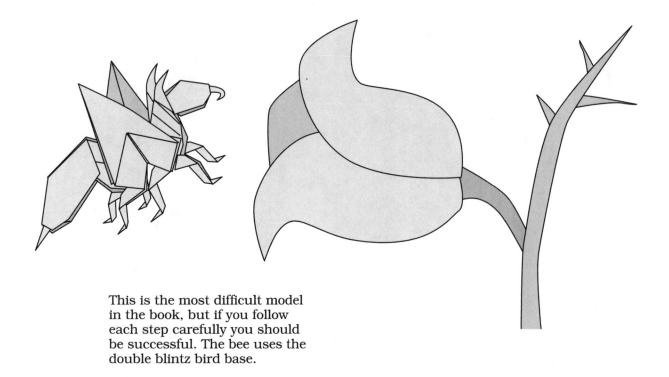

This is the most difficult model in the book, but if you follow each step carefully you should be successful. The bee uses the double blintz bird base.

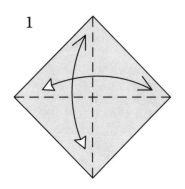

1

Fold and unfold along the diagonals.

2

Fold the corners to the center.

3

Blintz again.

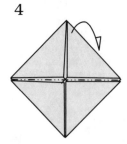

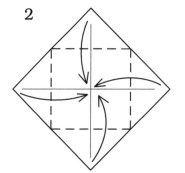

4

5

Squash-fold.

6

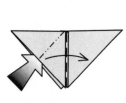

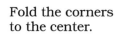

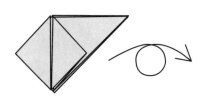

7

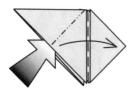

Squash-fold.

8

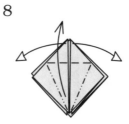

Petal-fold while pulling out
the corners. Repeat behind.
This is the same as steps 6–7
of the canary on page 69.

9

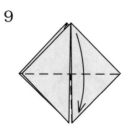

Repeat behind.

10

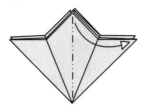

Unlock the paper.

11

Repeat step 10 on
the back and sides.

12

Fold and unfold.

13

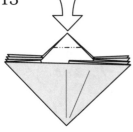

Sink.

14

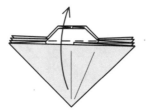

Repeat step 14 on
the back and sides.

15

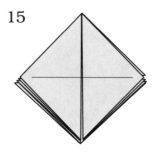

16

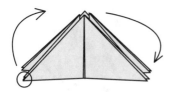

Note there is an inner
flap in each of the four
corners. Rotate.

17

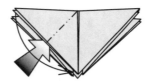

Squash-fold.

18

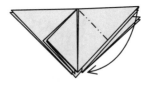

Repeat step 17 on
the right and behind.

Bee 117

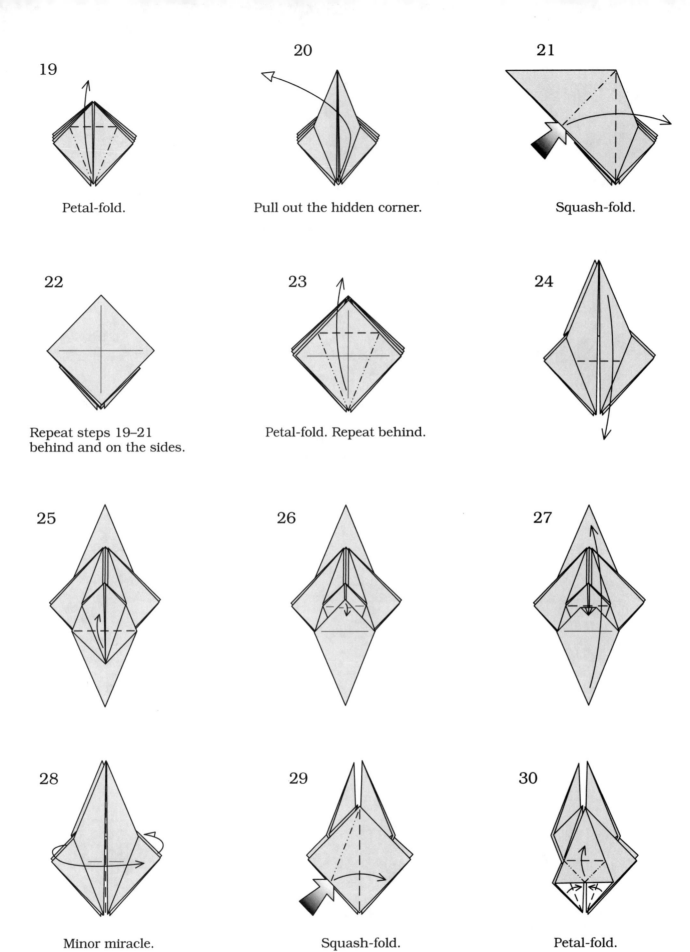

19

Petal-fold.

20

Pull out the hidden corner.

21

Squash-fold.

22

Repeat steps 19–21 behind and on the sides.

23

Petal-fold. Repeat behind.

24

25

26

27

28

Minor miracle.

29

Squash-fold.

30

Petal-fold.

30

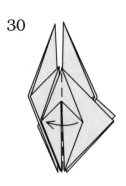

Repeat behind.

31

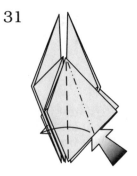

Squash-fold.
Repeat behind.

32

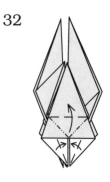

Petal-fold.
Repeat behind.

33

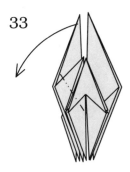

Reverse-fold.

34

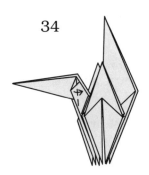

Repeat behind.

35

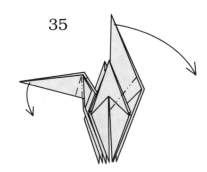

Crimp-fold at the head.
Reverse-fold the tail.

36

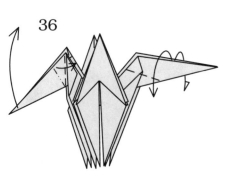

Crimp-fold at the head.
Outside-reverse-fold the tail.

37

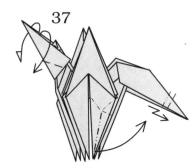

Outside-reverse-fold at the
head, crimp-fold the tail,
and double-rabbit-ear the
leg. Repeat behind.

38

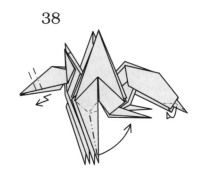

Repeat behind.

39

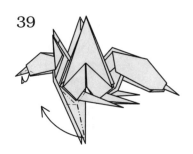

Repeat behind.

40

Repeat behind.

41

Bee

Afterthoughts

After folding the models shown here there are many ways to continue to enjoy origami. You can look for local origami groups, which are cropping up in many places. Or if you want, you can start one. Libraries are common meeting places.

Another possibility is to join OrigamiUSA. Among its many services, OrigamiUSA holds an annual origami convention where hundreds of folders gather for a few days to learn, share, and meet each other.

For more practice developing the skills you have learned in this book, you might look at the following books:

Origami Sculptures—24 models including dogs, horse, bison, panda, walrus from a dollar bill, peacock, geometric shapes, insects.

Prehistoric Origami—24 models including tyrannosaurus, apatosaurus, pterodactylus, triceratops, stegosaurus.

Origami Sea Life, Robert Lang, co-author—38 creatures including whales, mollusks, fishes, echinoderms, crustaceans.

African Animals in Origami—24 models including crocodile, gorilla, rhinoceros, hippopotamus, zebra, giraffe.

Origami Inside-Out—25 models dealing with the white and colored side including geometric shapes, Canada goose, spotted cow, chess board and chess pieces.

North American Animals in Origami , with contributions by Fumiaki Kawahata—25 models including cacti, beaver, owls, deer, raccoon, bison, musk ox, moose.

Mythological Creatures and the Chinese Zodiac in Origami—26 models including the 12 animals of the Chinese zodiac (rat, ox, tiger, rabbit, dragon, and others) along with unicorn, pegasus, three-headed dragon.

Books can be ordered from OrigamiUSA or Dover. Addresses are given in the introduction.